THIS BOOK IS THE LAST DATE STAM

BECOME
A FLY FISHER

Books by the same author

Flies That Catch Trout
The Upstream Wet Fly
Fly Fisher's Logbook

BECOME
A FLY FISHER

Terry Lawton

ROBERT HALE • LONDON

© Terry Lawton 2013
First published in Great Britain 2013

ISBN 978-0-7198-0619-3

Robert Hale Limited
Clerkenwell House
Clerkenwell Green
London EC1R 0HT

www.halebooks.com

All photographs by the author except:
Pages 11, 17, 68, 71, 79, 82, 85, 95, 102, 111, 113 Jérôme Philipon
Pages 35, 103, 107 Tim Gaunt-Baker
Page 14 Gustav Lawton

A catalogue record for this book is available from the British Library

2 4 6 8 10 9 7 5 3 1

Designed by Eurodesign
Printed in Singapore by Craft Print International Ltd

Contents

Acknowledgements

Thanks to Juliet Pennell for being a patient pupil and model and
to Sally Acloque who fishes because she wants to and not
because her husband encouraged her to.

Many thanks to Tim Gaunt-Baker (www.norfolkflyfishing.com)
for all his help with the chapter on casting and much other
sound advice. And to Snowbee (UK) Ltd (www.snowbee.co.uk)
for use of illustrations of fly line profiles and help with how fly
lines are made.

Introduction

There are many fishing books that can show a would-be angler how to cast a fly, and many that can teach you how to catch a trout. But there is a world of difference between casting a fly and catching fish and being able to call yourself a fisherman or woman. I know from personal experience of guiding anglers of different abilities and experience that many of them, even those who have fished for some years and claim to be quite experienced, have remarkably little understanding of what is involved in actually 'fishing' a stretch of river, as opposed to simply standing on the bank and casting to a feeding fish.

This book takes a new and different approach from most of the usual 'how to' books on fly fishing. Many titles assume some prior knowledge or understanding of fly fishing. This book does not. But just as important it does not 'dumb down' the subject. A lot of books for beginners to the sport spend many pages extolling the wonderful and interesting history of fly fishing. But is this of any real interest to the tyro angler? Someone who is interested in learning to play golf or tennis and buys a book on the subject will want to get on and start playing and would not expect to be told the history of the game. Once you have started to master the basics of fly fishing there will be plenty of time to read and learn about the history of the sport.

Become a Fly Fisher guides and instructs the would-be fly angler from the basic premise of why we fish for trout with flies, through buying and setting-up their tackle, to practical fishing sessions and catching fish. The book will help to demystify the sport without making the reader believe that he or she should expect to catch a bucket-full of fish every time they go fishing. Yes, we all want to catch fish but there will be many days when the fishing is hard and to catch just one fish will be a real success. Once you have got an understanding of the basics, if you then find that you are not able to fish regularly for a year or two, you will always be able to take it up again in due course. While tackle and flies may change, the basic skills do not.

This book contains plenty of essential, practical information but not so much that it will overwhelm the reader. It identifies and presents the necessary skills to be learnt and developed in an approachable and easy to understand way. For example, knots are introduced as and where they are needed as well as being gathered together in a separate chapter (where they can be found easily) towards the end of the book. As the tyro angler's knowledge and skills develop, this will help them gain confidence. Confidence, which is so important to successful fly fishing, can only be gained through actually going fishing and spending time trying to catch fish.

The book promotes the real joys and pleasures of fly fishing and a day on the water, whether river or stillwater, out in the country and away from daily cares and worries, for individuals, families and young people. Fishing at dawn on a summer morning as the sun rises and the mist clears from the river can be magical. You may get a fall of spinners that hatched the evening before or even during the night. At dusk, as the sun sets and mist rises off the river, darkness starts to descend and distant owls can be heard calling with a mix of hoots and the screeches of barn owls.

Even some long-time fly fishers find fishing nymphs impossibly difficult. But for those who learn how to do it the rewards are often substantial

There will be wonderful sounds of birdsong and wildlife in the bushes and trees and undergrowth on a warm, still summer's evening. Damsels and dragonflies will be hovering and darting over the river and in and out of the reeds at the river's edge. Sometimes a damsel will attack a Mayfly that has just taken flight, or a trout will leap from the water to consume a flying damsel.

If stillwater fishing or fly tying do not seem to have an appeal at this stage, don't worry as you can ignore these chapters (which stand by themselves) and perhaps read them later on. But learning to tie your own flies and catch fish with them adds to the overall appreciation and enjoyment of fly fishing.

People should not be put off taking up fly fishing by those who would have you believe that it is a hard, incomprehensible and inaccessible sport. But it is a challenging, stimulating, very pleasing and satisfying way to catch trout and grayling. Although I have concentrated on fly fishing for trout, these skills will provide a very solid foundation on which to build the necessary extra skills if you have the opportunity to fish for grayling. With a thorough grounding in fly fishing for trout in rivers and streams, the ambitious angler can then learn how to fish for sea trout and steelhead, salmon, coarse fish such as carp and pike and even try saltwater fly fishing.

Successful fly fishing can often be a question of being in the right place at the right time. Being on the river when a hatch starts and the fish begin to rise for example. Some anglers like to be busy and keep casting on the move, casting to likely spots in anticipation of finding a hungry fish. Others fish much more slowly and perhaps more methodically, waiting for a fish to rise so that they can cast to it. It doesn't matter which approach suits your character as neither is completely right or completely wrong. Each to his own.

Fly fishing can be a strange sport. Once you have got to the stage when you can catch a fish you will then want to catch as many fish as you can. However, once you reach that stage and start to understand and appreciate the subtleties of the sport, if the fish are too easy to catch (it can happen) then the fishing can seem lacking in challenge. But if the fishing is *so* hard and the fish *so* difficult to catch that you don't catch even one, then that can be very disappointing. What we all want is a day when the fishing is hard enough to present a worthwhile challenge, but easy enough to be able to catch a fish or two.

When you have read this book I hope that you will realize that there is more to fly fishing than just catching fish. There will be days when fish are not feeding, or you cannot get one to rise to your fly or even take a look at it, but that is all part of fly fishing. But the next time that you go fishing and have some success will help to make the less-good days bearable.

* * * *

Note: When referring to the right-hand or left-hand bank of a river the convention is that the banks are designated when looking downstream, regardless of which bank you are standing on. So when fishing upstream, a right-handed angler would choose to fish on the (true) right-hand bank (TRHB) – so his or her casting arm is next to the water and a left-hander would choose the 'true' left-hand bank (TLHB) for the same reason.

CHAPTER ONE

How to seduce trout

Fly fishing is about trying to outwit or seduce a fish into taking your artificial fly. It is based on the fundamental principle of casting an artificial fly to a fish feeding on natural flies. Fly fishing is also one of the very best ways to enjoy and get a better understanding of nature.

Fly fishing is not always the easiest way to catch trout or grayling but it is most certainly the most challenging and satisfying. If all you want to do is catch or remove as many fish as possible from a river or lake, then fish with a worm or bunch of maggots. You will achieve your objective, but will there be any sense of achievement or pleasure at having outwitted a fish in its own environment? Although there are still rules and regulations prescribing how, where and when you can fish for trout (some club rules are more restrictive than others) fortunately today we are not so hide-bound or dominated by dry-fly purists who used to insist that the only sporting way to catch a trout was to cast an artificial dry-fly, imitating the natural fly a fish was feeding on, to a fish that you could see rising to and feeding on flies on the surface. This is the way that some people still fish and that is their choice and they should be left to enjoy their own restricted way of fishing. But following such a narrow approach is to deny yourself the chance of catching fish that are not rising regularly, or are feeding below the surface. And trout find by far the greatest part of their food below the surface: nymphs, shrimps, larvae, snails, small fish and so on (see Chapter 5).

Nymph fishing is a very successful way of catching fish because trout can feed easily and safely below the surface. This wild brown trout has been caught on a nymph

Jérôme Philpon

Once you can cast your fly accurately – so that it lands where you want it to – you will be able to catch fish fairly consistently

Chalk streams and limestone spring creeks, with their gin-clear water and luxuriant weed growth, can provide some of the best and most challenging fly fishing

When fly fishing for trout you should try to fish the method and associated fly type that matches where the fish you want to catch are feeding (on the surface or below) and what they may be feeding on. Some people may consider this to be a somewhat restrictive and old-fashioned concept but there is nothing to say that you cannot change your ideas or approach once you know what you are doing. There are two main ways of fly fishing: dry-fly fishing using 'dry' flies which are designed to float on the water's surface (see Chapter 7), and fishing with nymphs which are 'wet' and fished below the surface (see Chapter 8). Dry-fly fishing is the best-known and more popular partly because it is much more visual than nymph fishing as the fly is in view all the time and anglers like to see a fish rise to their fly and, partly it can be argued, because it is easier than nymph fishing. So it makes sense to set out to learn to fish the dry fly before moving on to

fishing nymphs. However, anglers who restrict themselves to the dry fly only will find that they miss a lot of good sport because fish that are feeding *below* the surface can be (but are not always) reluctant to rise to a fly that is being fished *on* the surface. Trout in particular do not always do what we expect, or confirm to stereotypes. As they don't read fishing books, always be prepared for the unexpected.

The fly fisher must be able to get his or her fly to within reach of a feeding fish to stand any chance of catching it. This does not mean being able to make ultra-long casts but, rather, *accurate* casts – accuracy is far more important than distance. You need to be able to make a number of accurate casts, with your fly landing on target with each one. Concentrate on learning to cast accurately: distance can and will follow in due course. Even when fishing stillwaters, where longer casts are normal, the angler who can cast

THE LEGAL STUFF

In many countries there are open and closed seasons for fly fishing, dictated primarily by when fish are likely to breed and sometimes by the weather or even a combination of these factors. But in some countries there is no closed season. Trout breed during the winter months whereas grayling breed in the spring and early summer. As closed seasons do vary, it is best to check locally if it is legal to go fishing. In the UK the trout fishing season can open as early as 15 March and close on 29 October, but some rivers will not open until 1 April, or even May, and may close at the end of September or the middle of October. Dates depend on the location and type of river and local by-laws.

Where there are grayling, fishing for them is allowed during the closed season for trout. Fishing for grayling in a classic chalk stream such as the river Test is an inexpensive way to fish such a river.

Although there are no legally obligated closed seasons for stillwaters, some will close during the winter and you will need to check with the fishery. Some stillwaters may also close during periods of very hot weather and in the winter if the water is frozen.

As well as observing closed seasons, there are varying requirements for licences. In the UK it is a legal requirement to have an Environment Agency licence for trout if you are aged 12 or over. To fish for non-migratory trout (not sea trout) you will need a rod licence for non-migratory trout and coarse fish. You can buy one from post offices in England and Wales or on-line from the Environment Agency website http://www.environment-agency.gov.uk Other countries have systems of local, regional or national permits. Scotland has no national licensing system.

It must be noted that while an Environment Agency licence gives you the right to use a fishing rod and line, it does not give you a right to fish. You must have the permission of the owner or tenant of the fishing rights before starting to fish. The same thing applies in Scotland.

accurately will still catch fish; often as many as the man or woman who can reach fish much further away. Making short casts to feeding fish ensures that you are closer to the action when a fish takes your fly.

Fly fishing is an active pursuit – more so on rivers than is often the case on small stillwaters – as it involves making progress along a riverbank, looking for fish to cast to or places that might hold fish. There is no sitting on a chair watching an unmoving float. The fly fisher is mobile and so doesn't want to be burdened with any more 'stuff' than is essential. Once smitten it is difficult not to start acquiring rods, reels, ever more flies, fly boxes to put them in and all the other paraphernalia, but it is possible to start with the bare minimum of suitable tackle – we will look at everything that you need to get started in the next chapter – and add to it gradually. Family, friends and relatives will never again wonder what to buy the tyro fly fisher for Christmas and birthday presents.

Rivers where we fish for trout are known as trout streams or, in specific areas of the UK, as chalk streams. Trout are to be found in rivers and streams where the water is clean and of a high quality; grayling thrive only in cool water of the highest quality as they are sensitive to pollution. The term chalk stream does not mean that all such waters are streams or small rivers, nor does it imply that trout are found only in chalk streams. The world-famous River Test is a chalk stream but, for much of its length it is, in fact, a wide and substantial river. A chalk stream is a stream or river for which springs are the main source of water, these being fed by water in the aquifers deep in the layers of chalk that stretch from Normandy in France, under the English Channel, through Hampshire up to Norfolk and on through Lincolnshire to end in Yorkshire. (The limestone spring creeks in the USA share similar character-istics.) The water in a chalk stream can usually be described as gin clear so that everything is easy to see; weed growth is often prolific (weed harbours food for the fish as well as providing protection) and many chalk streams flow through some of the most attractive scenery. Good rivers and good scenery tend to go together and these qualities are not restricted to chalk streams, as many examples of the other main type of river, rain-fed, have their sources in mountains and moorlands.

Although trout are, in the main, opportunistic feeders and will take a well-presented artificial fly, either a dry or a nymph, there are times when they can be very fussy. This fussiness is often described as feeding selectively. This might be because more than one fly is hatching at the same time and some fish are feeding on one fly and other fish on another. Or it might be that they are feeding on nymphs very close to the surface, or insects as they are hatching in the surface film

where they make an easy meal as they struggle free of the nymphal shuck.

If more than one fly is hatching or fish seem to be feeding selectively, it can be a real intellectual challenge to work out exactly what is going on. If there is a noticeable difference in the size of flies, fish will sometimes take the smaller in preference

A pretty little wild brown trout about to be returned to the water. It should be none the worse from the experience of being caught and released, but no doubt a little wiser

A section of a classic French chalk stream, the Risle in Normandy

Gustav Lawton

to the bigger ones. Fly fishing in such circumstances is far from simply selecting a 'nice looking' fly and chucking it out on the water. Coming to terms with selective feeding is all part of the fun of learning how to seduce a trout into taking your fly.

Many fly anglers, once they know what they are doing, prefer to fish on their own, but those new to the sport are encouraged to spend time with a knowledgeable friend who can provide guidance and encouragement at, all being well, opportune moments and revive flagging spirits if necessary. On some rivers two friends will be able to fish close together without getting in each other's way, but on other rivers you may need to give each other plenty of space and a good stretch of water to fish.

When this happens, meeting after a while to share a coffee or have lunch together is an ideal opportunity to compare experiences.

Fly fishing demands a high level of concen-

tration so it is very easy to forget about the stresses and strains of daily life and lose all sense of time. You may want to take a mobile phone with you in case of an emergency, but try not to turn it on unless you have to. Be warned: given a degree of aptitude, good powers of observation and real interest, fly fishing will very soon become an all-absorbing passion. Moving about the riverbank or beside a stillwater slowly and quietly it is surprising how close you can get to all sorts of wildlife. On some rivers you might be fortunate enough to see a water vole or an otter, possibly even a stoat hunting the river margins for eggs or an unwary moorhen. Barn owls can be seen quartering water meadows at dusk or hunting for food for their young during the day, and towards the end of the season you may even hear the bark of a rutting stag. As well as wildlife there will often be plenty of pretty or interesting flowers to be seen and perhaps some blackberries ripe for eating. If the fishing is slow

When you can fish alongside a companion, taking it in turns to fish, you can learn a lot by watching whether and how a fish reacts to your companion's fly. The performance of breathable waders, as worn by these two anglers, is much improved by wearing 'wicking' clothing – rather than cotton – which helps take the moisture away from your skin

A good day's fishing doesn't have to be all action. On a warm, sunny day it is nice to be able to put your rod down, relax and take in the scenery

or you feel like a rest, sitting on the bank or a well-placed riverside seat will soon recharge your batteries.

Once you find yourself getting more and more involved with fly fishing, you may consider joining a fishing club. Clubs and syndicates operate at different (financial) levels depending on where they are and the type and quality of fishing available to members. Joining a club may involve paying an entrance fee and a subscription for an annual rod, or part rod, or an annual subscription only. Some of the big and expensive clubs will probably employ a river-keeper who will look after the river. But smaller clubs often look to their members for help with work on the river. River work is a very interesting and satisfying way to get to know a river really well, although it can be hard going especially if there is a lot of weed that needs to be cut. But river work that involves getting into the river is the best way to find out where the shallows are and

Fishing a small trout stream under an overhead canopy of trees is a real challenge. But when you catch a fish the pleasure and sense of achievement will be that much greater

the hidden deep spots. You will meet other club members and find out their favourite places to fish and usually learn quite a lot about how to fish the river.

Fly tying is another aspect of the sport that many will take up. It's a great way of getting through the close season in a creative way. The first flies that you tie may well be rough and ready, but once your confidence starts to grow you will soon be able to produce flies of an acceptable quality. You can find out how to tie flies in Chapter 13.

Dominic Lawson wrote in *The Sunday Times* (8 April 2012) about 'the extraordinary acceleration of life created by the advent of electronic communication' which had 'only made this terror worse'. He continued: 'In theory, such developments ought to have given us hours of extra leisure time in which we could and even should indulge in our more contemplative hobbies: fishing for example.' Towards the end of his article in support of his desire to 'escape from the tyranny of time' he quoted the following passage from Winifred Gallagher's book *Rapt: Attention and the Focused Life:* 'Paying rapt attention, whether to a trout stream or a novel, a do-it-yourself project or a prayer, increases your capacity for concentration and lifts your spirits, but, more important, it simply makes you feel that life is worth living.' Does anyone need a better reason to learn to become a fly fisher and a seducer of trout?

Once started on the life-affirming process of becoming a fly fisher you will never stop learning. It is a rare day on a river when something different or unusual does not happen. Fly fishing is a sport that rewards those who are able to spend time learning to cast well and getting to know a piece of water in all its moods and the different seasons, whether a river or a stillwater. A knot-tying website that I found recently had some general advice on tying fishing knots that included 'Fish often!' and 'Take a kid fishing!' Once you start making progress towards becoming a fly fisher, in part by 'fishing often', you will soon be able, and want, to pass on your knowledge and 'take a kid [of any age] fishing'.

Jérôme Philipor

The more time that you can spend on or in a river the better you will be able to fish

CHAPTER TWO

What you need for fly fishing

Buying everything you need to start fly fishing does not have to cost a lot of money. You can spend a lot on buying big brand names where you are buying the name, or you can buy good quality and very serviceable tackle for a more modest outlay.

Although it is possible – and all too easy – to spend a lot of money on a fly rod, reel, waders, clothing and all the other equipment, it is not necessary. Owning and using the best tackle does give great pleasure but carefully selected less expensive equipment will work just as well, as long as everything is in balance. Some items of tackle are bought infrequently and will provide many years of service. Others will need replacing, or possibly upgrading, during the season. So while it is not necessary to spend a lot of money on a starter outfit, beware of buying things just because they seem to be very cheap.

Fly fishers tend towards one of two types: tackle junkies who are unhappy unless they are kitted-out – and weighed down – with every bit of tackle imaginable, and those who favour a minimalist approach, taking the least amount of only essential equipment with them. A minimalist can convert to a tackle junkie quite easily but for a junkie to convert to the minimalist approach will mean suffering withdrawal symptoms and thoughts of 'if only I had got such and such with me'.

Some people will be happy with the first rod, reel and line that they buy and will use them for a long time. Others will soon realize the shortcomings of their first purchases and look to buy a better reel and fly line and a rod with a different action. Although it is possible to buy rods and

reels that are thoroughly serviceable for little money, it is worth remembering that if you do decide to buy a better rod or reel, your first purchases will always be available should you ever need a spare rod. Fly lines tend not to last so long as they are easily damaged by standing on them or getting them tangled in knots. They tend to need replacing more frequently.

The fly rod

A modern fly rod is a wondrous piece of equipment with extraordinary strength and a great ability to flex, combined in a package that weighs far less than might be imagined. A fly rod is an amalgam of computer-aided design, some of the latest synthetic materials – particularly carbon fibre – and very advanced manufacturing techniques. Rods are made in a range of lengths, each one to be used with a specific weight of fly line. The name of the rod-maker, the length of the rod and the correct weight of fly line to be used with it can all be found marked on the rod blank just above the handle.

Rods and reels can be bought in a range of styles and even colours. Here are four mid- or large-arbor reels and two with traditional spools. Only two of the six are set up to be wound with the right hand

All rods have information that shows you the maker's name, the model of rod, its length and the correct weight of line to use with it

Right The design and manufacture of multi-piece rods is so good that it is all but impossible to know how many joints a rod has when fishing

You can pay as little or as much as you can afford for a fly rod. But simply buying a rod made by the best – and usually most expensive – maker may not result in a rod suited to the beginner. A serviceable fly rod can be bought for a price that is about a twentieth of the cost of a top-end rod. Why is there so much difference? With a top-end rod you are paying a premium for the name, the best design, the use of the latest materials and manufacturing techniques, and a quality of finish that should set such a rod a long way apart from one at the other end of the cost scale. The cheaper rods are made using less advanced materials and rod tapers (it is the taper of each section and the overall taper of a rod that makes it cast in the way that it does), and will be assembled with less care, using cheaper fittings – reel seat, rod rings – which is very often most noticeable in the quality of cork used for the rod handle. Cheap cork is rather coarse and often has holes in it which have to be filled. Cheap rods will cast a fly, play and land many a fish, but with less pleasure of ownership and enjoyment in use than their top-end counterparts. A top-end fly rod will cast a fly with far less effort than a less well-designed rod, or cast it much further for an equal amount of effort. Good rods are much more efficient than their cheaper counterparts. As so much of a day's fishing will be spent casting, it makes sense to buy a rod that you enjoy using and which has an action that works for you.

For many years the standard trout fly rod was made in two pieces: a butt, or bottom, section and a top section. Rods are usually sold in a cotton bag but sometimes with a hard protective tube as well. A two-piece rod is quick and easy to assemble as there is only the one joint connecting the two sections (the joints in fly rods are known as ferrules), but the length of the two sections makes such a rod inconvenient to store or put in a car boot. For a long time it was felt that the more joints, or sections, that a rod had, the

worse it would be to cast and fish with. Fortunately, modern rod design, materials and manufacturing techniques have shown this not to be a concern any more. Now multi-piece, or travel rods, are becoming ever more popular. These rods are made with four, five, six or even seven sections. They are invariably sold with a protective tube and usually a cotton bag as well, although some come in a tube with internal dividers and no rod bag. A rod with a bag and tube is more versatile as you can take the rod with you in its bag, without the tube, or put two rods in the same tube without them getting mixed up or damaged. The downside to a six- or seven-piece rod is the number of sections that have to be joined together (and taken apart at the end of the day) and aligned carefully.

Rods are made in different lengths, for different weights of fly line and, as already mentioned, with what are known as different actions. The newcomer to fly fishing will be well advised not to buy anything too extreme in either length or line weight. A 6 ft (1.8 m) rod with a very

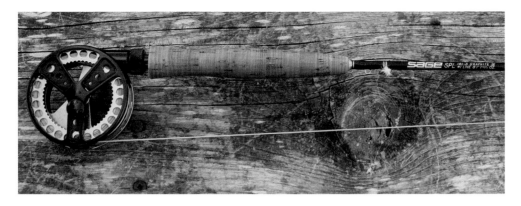

Short, light-line rods are fun to fish with but can be a liability if you are fishing a river with high bankside vegetation or wading a river with high banks where it can be difficult to keep your back cast high enough to avoid hooking the vegetation. They can also make life difficult on very windy days

light line – a #1, #2 or #3 weight – will provide a lot of pleasure and enjoyment for a competent angler who understands the limitations imposed by such tackle. A short rod will make life difficult when casting if there is a lot of vegetation on the bank, and also when managing your line on the water. It will also be challenging to use for casting into a strong wind. Should you hook a big fish you will have a much harder job bringing the fish to hand so that it can be released, or netted. The optimum length of rod for most river fishing is between 8 and 9 ft (2.45–2.75 m). Such a rod is long enough to be able to cast over high vegetation and manipulate the line on the water, but not so long that it is difficult to use in confined areas. Should you anticipate fishing small or medium-size rivers you might decide to go for an 8 ft or 8½ ft (2.45 or 2.6 m) rod. But if bigger rivers are likely to feature regularly, then a 9 ft (2.75 m) rod would be the right choice.

HOW FLY RODS ARE MADE – A BRIEF GUIDE

A carbon-fibre fly rod is made by wrapping a sheet of carbon fibre (called a prepreg as it is impregnated with a mixture of special resins), around a tapered steel mandrel and then baking it in an oven. The prepreg is reinforced with a scrim that is aligned perpendicular to the carbon fibres, which run lengthwise. The scrim is sandwiched between the layers of carbon fibre. It gives a rod hoop strength which stops the rod section from going oval when it bends. The resins used are usually trade secrets, with different manufacturers using their own special brews.

The steel mandrel is designed by the rod-maker, using a computer, and then machined to very precise tolerances. Various prototypes will be made in the search for the characteristics the designer is looking for. A multi-piece rod will have a separate mandrel for each section. The pieces of carbon fibre that are wrapped around each mandrel are cut to an exact and often intricate pattern. The intricacies of the pattern are there to create the desired taper and rod action. The mandrel is sprayed with a release agent so that it can be withdrawn from the finished tube. It is then laid along the edge of the carbon fibre-scrim sandwich and given one complete roll. It is essential that this first turn or roll is absolutely right and it is a job for an expert. The rest of the material is rolled onto the mandrel by industrial rolling machinery. The rolled blank is bound with heat-resistant polypropylene tape to hold it all together. The completed sections are then hung in an oven to cure. Once cured the mandrel is extracted using a pneumatic pull press and a specially sized die that fits the butt end of each blank section.

When the tape is removed from the blank it leaves a series of ridges running around the length of the blank. Sometimes these ridges are left for a natural finish, or they can be sanded away for rods that will have a smooth finish. Blanks that have been sanded are then painted, have ferrules fitted and are finally dipped in a permanent, protective epoxy coating which has to be allowed to cure for some hours in a dust-free environment for a perfect blemish-free finish.

The finished blanks are now ready to be fitted with all the components – handle, reel seat, rod rings – that turn a bare blank into a finished fly rod.

The next point to consider is line weight. To use a shooting analogy, if a twelve-bore is the most popular game gun, its angling equivalent would be a #5- or #6-weight line; a sixteen bore a #4-weight line and a twenty bore a #3 or #2 line. The best line weight for small and medium-size rivers is a #4 and for bigger waters a #5-weight or possibly a #6. Anything bigger and you risk being over-gunned. Long rods and heavy lines will soon become hard work and detract from the enjoyment; but if you fish in anything other than ideal conditions (with little or no wind) you will struggle to cast your fly to a fish any distance away with a short rod and very light line.

Rod action is something that obsesses far too many anglers. The would-be fly fisher needs to be aware of the fact that rods have different actions, but it is not until a number of different makes and model of rod have been test-cast that you can have any appreciation or understanding of what the different terms mean. The best way to start learning about rod action is to spend an hour with a casting instructor who can make available a range of rods for you to try, or go to a tackle shop that has facilities for you to try casting with different rods. Country sports fairs often provide casting tuition and an opportunity to try different fly rods.

Some of the bigger and better rod-makers sell rods designed for the beginner, with a responsive, progressive and forgiving 'through' action. This means that the rod will load or bend easily and mistakes in timing between the back cast and the forward cast will not be too disastrous. The beginner wants a rod with a medium and forgiving action. To use an equestrian analogy such a rod is comparable to a steady hunter who will get you across country without too many frights. A fast, or tip-action rod in which most of the bend when casting is towards the top of the rod, is much more akin to a 3-year-old colt who has the potential to win the Derby – extremely fast but not a reassuring ride for a novice!

If you anticipate or know that you are likely to spend most of your time fishing small stillwaters, then it would make good sense to consider buying a slightly longer and more powerful rod such as a 9 or 9½ ft (2.75 or 2.9 m) rod for a #5- or #6-weight line. It is unlikely that you would want anything more than a 10 ft (3 m) rod for a #7-weight line.

The important thing to make sure of is that your rod and line match and are in balance. All fly lines are made to a long-established standard – based on the weight of the first 30 ft (9.1 m) of line – so any make of #5 line will be similar to any other. This means that if you have a 5-weight rod it will be matched by any #5 make of line. Although most rods are designed to perform to their optimum with one weight of line, there are some rods that have a twin line rating, for example #6 or #7. This means that the rod can be fished with either a double taper #6 or weight-forward #7 line.

When you get your rod home for the first time, take it out of its tube and bag and check it over carefully. At the same time, remove the shrink wrap covering the handle. It is there only to keep the cork handle clean before it is sold. Leaving it on will make the rod handle slippery and difficult to hold firmly. And if you do not remove it, water will get behind it and discolour the cork.

Fly line

Although, for most river fly fishing, the only line that you need will be a floating line, the choice for the stillwater angler is more varied (see Chapter 9). As the name suggests, a floating line is designed to float on the surface of the water and not sink. Fly lines are made to float, to sink at a range of different speeds and to different depths, to hover just below the surface, and with tips that will sink. Many of them are designed for very specialized uses such as fishing nymphs or buzzers on stillwaters. To add to the confusion, lines can be designed for delicate presentations or to cast extreme distances, as well as for everyday use.

Lines are designed and made to very exacting tapers to produce optimum performance from the line, whether it be for making delicate casts at short range with small dry flies or presenting bigger, heavier flies at long range. Fly lines are designed with one of two types of taper: double taper, where both ends have the same taper and

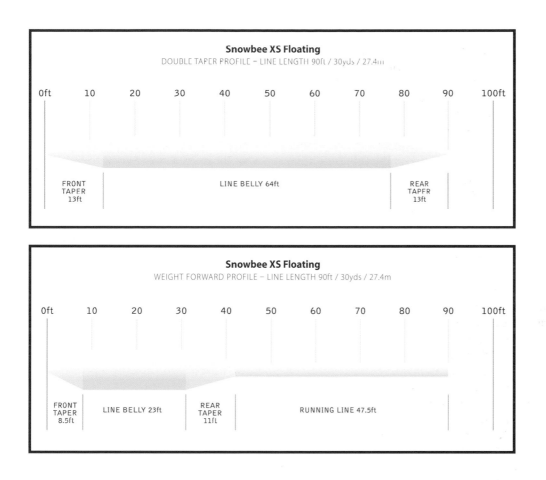

Snowbee XS Floating
DOUBLE TAPER PROFILE – LINE LENGTH 90ft / 30yds / 27.4m

0ft   10   20   30   40   50   60   70   80   90   100ft

FRONT TAPER 13ft   LINE BELLY 64ft   REAR TAPER 13ft

Snowbee XS Floating
WEIGHT FORWARD PROFILE – LINE LENGTH 90ft / 30yds / 27.4m

0ft   10   20   30   40   50   60   70   80   90   100ft

FRONT TAPER 8.5ft   LINE BELLY 23ft   REAR TAPER 11ft   RUNNING LINE 47.5ft

the maximum thickness of the line is in the middle, and forward taper, where the thickness and main weight of the line is at the leading or forward end and the rest of the line is a thin running line. Some companies make lines with tapers designed for the newcomer to fly fishing. It has long been felt that a double-taper line is the best for making precise, delicate casts so that the fly, leader and line land on the surface of the water with the least disturbance. This may be true for the competent caster, but for many a weight-forward line can be easier to cast and will allow the beginner to make better casts and thus better presentations.

All types of lines are named using an industry-standard combination of letters and numbers. The most important letters to know are WF (weight forward), DT (double taper), and F (floating). To make sure that you buy the correct weight of line for your rod, check the information on the rod just above the handle. If you are buying a #4-weight forward floating line, the box will be marked WF4F along with the maker's name, the colour and length of the line. To make

It's easy to check that you have bought the right type of fly line by checking the label on the box

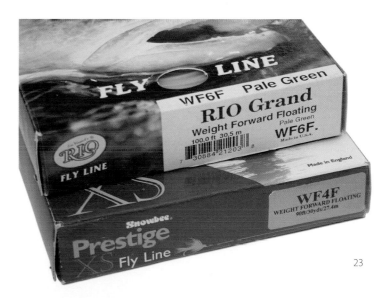

Although many experienced anglers do not like brightly coloured lines, they make life easier for the beginner as they are much easier to see in the air when casting, and on the water

things extra clear, WFF is usually spelt out: Weight Forward Floating.

Lines are available in almost every colour from clear (for specialist uses only), through white, ivory, sand, olive, green, yellow, willow, blue, peach, orange and fluorescent or hi-viz orange, and in various combinations. White and very pale lines are best avoided as they get so dirty, but this does show the importance of cleaning a line regularly and re-dressing it (with the product supplied with the line). Using a clean line is one of the best aids to casting easily and well.

So, what is the best line to buy? Chose an all-round or general-purpose, weight-forward, floating line (of the right weight) made by one of the leading line manufacturers such as Cortland, Rio or Scientific Anglers (in alphabetical order) or all-round tackle-makers such as Snowbee, Orvis

HOW A FLY LINE IS MADE

Fly lines comprise two main components: an inner core and an outer coating. Each and every fly line manufacturer has their own recipes and manufacturing procedures, most of which are highly secret. Both the components contribute to a line's performance in different ways. Today's fly lines are an intriguing mix of science and practical fishing: the boys in the lab come up with lots of ideas and the fly fishermen try them out to test which work the best. In order that a floating line will float, it must have a low specific gravity. One thing that all manufacturers strive for is the lowest specific gravity, which will result in a line that will float as high as possible for as long as possible.

Many different types of core material are used for making fly lines, including various kinds of braided nylon or monofilament and extruded monofilament. The core provides the line's strength which, perhaps surprisingly, is of little or no concern to fly fishermen, who simply accept that a fly line is more than strong enough for its intended use. Stiffer cores are used for lines that will be used in warm and hot climates and softer, more flexible cores for cold weather use when fly lines can tend to stiffen and be difficult to handle. To ensure that the core material is completely dry before the next stage of production, they are often placed in a dehumidifier to extract any moisture. For a line to cast properly and last, the

core must be coated evenly so that it is in the centre of the coating. Before the outer coating can be applied, the core is primed with a special adhesive to ensure that the coating bonds completely. This process can be done by drawing the core material through a bath of liquid adhesive. Priming the core successfully has an important effect on the durability of a line.

The basis of a fly line coating is liquid plastisol, to which are added such things as plasticizers, silicone, lubricants including Teflon, and glass microspheres that make a floating line float. Some manufacturers have moved on from using microspheres in floating lines – now old technology – to incorporating specially developed chemicals that can only be used with a new manufacturing technique that bonds an extra-buoyant undercoating to a super-smooth and slick outer coating. The result is said to be lines that will float even higher in the water. The coating creates the desired taper and all the desirable qualities such as lubrication and shootability, low memory and floatability, for floating lines, or varying sink rates for sinking lines.

Manufacturers who finish their lines with built-in loops now make these loops and, once that process is completed, the lines are ready for a final inspection before packing ready for sale.

or Hardy/Greys. Buy one from the lower end of their price range to start with in case you damage it, and in a muted colour, but one that you can still see.

Backing

You will also have to buy some thin woven polyester yarn known as backing. This backing line, which is often a highly visible colour, is sold on spools of various lengths from 50 m upwards, with a breaking strain of either 20 lbs (9.07 kg), which is quite strong enough for trout fishing, or 30 lbs (13.6 kg). Backing is inexpensive so it is worth buying more than you need initially as this will mean that you will have some for another reel or extra spool. The main reason for fitting backing is that fly lines are usually only 30 yards (27.5 m) long, so the backing provides extra line in readiness for the magical day when you hook a fish big and powerful enough for you to see the end of your fly line. A second reason for backing is that when many reels had very small diameter spools, or arbors, filling the reel with backing increased the diameter of the spool. This meant that the fly line was not wrapped in quite such small turns and so there would be slightly fewer coils to

cause tangles and perhaps get stuck in a rod ring or guide.

Fly reel

Some fly fishers argue that a reel is only a means of holding a fly line neatly and tidily. Many reels are over-engineered for much trout fishing, fitted as they are with drag systems that could check the progress of a very large salmon. While there is some truth in this, using and owning a well-designed and made reel is a pleasure and part of the joy of fly fishing.

Alternatively, an inexpensive moulded graphite reel is a good starter reel for someone young who may damage or not look after an expensive reel properly. A word of warning, however: these reels can break if dropped on something hard such as concrete or a road. As with a fly rod, it will always be very useful to have a spare reel.

Whatever type or make of reel you buy, it must have a simple click drag system to prevent the spool running free and causing over-runs, even if it does not have a more expensive adjustable drag system.

A good trout reel should have either a mid-

Good-quality tackle and equipment that works properly, and need not be very expensive, will make fly fishing a little easier and more enjoyable

sized or large arbor so that when the line is wound onto it, the coils will not be too small and tight. It wants to be as light as possible (but reducing weight does cost money) and the right size for the line weight of your fly rod.

Stillwater anglers should consider a cassette- or cartridge-type reel. These reels have a quick-change spool system which means that you can have a spare spool with a different type of line on it and can change lines quickly should you need to. These reels are usually supplied with one or two spare cassettes, which are much cheaper than spare spools. They were developed to meet the needs of still-water anglers who will often have a range of different fly lines with them.

The drag on this reel is tightened or slackened by turning the large central knob. If you set it too tight you will have trouble pulling the line off your reel when you want to cast. The # 3/4 shows the line weights for which this reel is suitable.

Looking after an expensive fly reel by keeping it clean and properly lubricated will ensure that it performs well for many years

Reels with open cages are much easier to remove in order to replace the spool without risking trapping and damaging your fly line or leader. With a full or closed cage, as here, the line has to pass between the cage and the spool when removing the spool and when refitting it. This reel has a notch cut into the back of the spool, so that the line doesn't get trapped

Leaders

A leader provides a low-visibility connection between the end of the fly line and the fly. It must be tapered as it is an important part of presenting a fly well, because it transmits a decreasing flow of energy to the fly. Leaders can be made in several ways: by tying together varying lengths of monofilament, of decreasing breaking strain; from one length of tapered mono; or from a number of furled threads. The diameter of the thick, or butt, end is usually around 60 per cent of that of the end of the fly line.

The average leader, whether knotted or knotless, does not have a very long life, but it is possible to make a leader that, with care, will last a whole season.

You can do this by buying what is known as a floating poly leader, which is a leader made in a similar way to a fly line with a thin, continuous monofilament core and a tapered outer coating. These leaders are made in two lengths, 5 ft (1.5 m)

The life of a leader can be extended by fitting a tiny stainless steel ring to the thin end, to which you attach a tippet. This means that you do not have to cut the leader each time you change tippet. A leader to be used for nymph fishing can also be fitted with an indicator

or 10 ft (3 m). A 5 ft (1.5 m) leader is the one to go for. There will be a loop at the thick end, and the thin end will be just the exposed mono core. Start by removing the manufacturer's loop as these are too heavy and bulky. With a sharp knife, or scalpel, remove a short length of the outer coating to expose the inner core. Be careful doing this; it is very easy to cut the core as well. Now tie a loop, using a surgeon's loop knot (see below), as close to the end of the outer core as you can. At the thin end you want to attach a tiny leader ring. These are stainless steel rings 1 mm in diameter. You can attach one to the leader using a tucked half blood knot (see below). With a loop on the end of your leader, you can attach it to your fly line using the loop-to-loop connection (see page 173). You will also need to add a tippet – a sacrificial length of monofilament between the end of the leader and the fly – use a tucked half blood knot again.

Leaders with loops at each end reduce the number of knots needed. Every knot eliminated is one potential weakness done way with

TYING A SURGEON'S LOOP

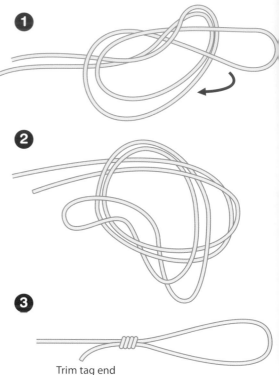

Trim tag end

1 Take about 4 in (10 cm) of the end of the line and use it to make a loop.
2 Hold the loop with one hand and use the other to tie an overhand knot with the two lines.
3 Pass the end of the loop through the loop you have just made.
4 Moisten the knot and, still holding the two lines in one hand, pass something smooth and round through the loop and pull firmly to tighten the knot.
5 Complete the knot by trimming the tag end.

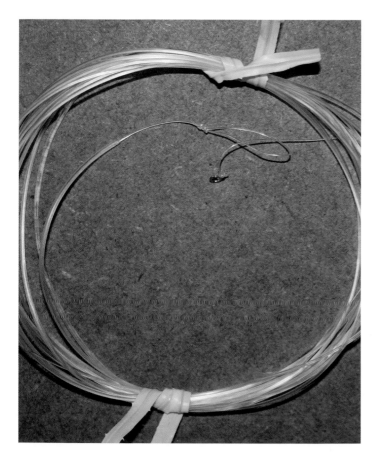

TYING A EUGENE BEND

The Eugene bend is a strong, foolproof knot that is easy to tie and works best with monofilament lines of up to 12 lb (5.5 kg) breaking strain. The knot is almost as strong as the breaking strain of the line – *some knots provide less than one hundred per cent of the line strength and are best avoided*. It is as foolproof as any fishing knot can be. It is no more wasteful than other knots for similar purposes. Because this knot is tied using monofilament only, it must be lubricated with saliva, or water, to make it slide easily and prevent friction causing heat which could damage the line. As you tighten the knot a slight click, or pop, tells you that the knot is set tight.

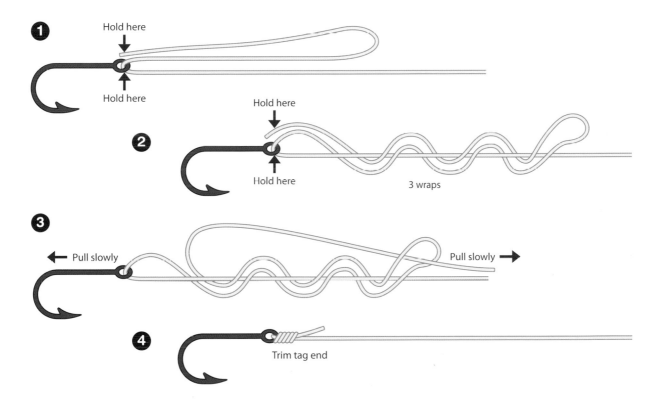

1 Thread about 6 in (15 cm) of tippet through the hook eye, from the underside of the eye, and then run it back up alongside standing main line.
2 Hold the two lines together with your thumb and finger and form a long loop by taking the tag end back towards the hook. Hold all the lines and hook eye between your thumb and index finger.
3 Wrap the loop you have just formed around the standing line three times.
4 Pass the tag end through the loop and then, using the finger and thumb of your right hand, pull the tag end until the knot is just snug – not tight – and the loops are small enough not to slip over the eye of the hook.
5. Wet the knot and pull slowly until the knot seats against the hook eye. When done correctly, you will feel and hear a reassuring slight click or 'pop' that tells you that the knot is tight. A properly tied and seated knot will have the tag end forming a very pronounced 'V' with the standing line.

Finish the knot by trimming the tag end.

Tucked half blood knot

The tucked half blood knot is one of a number of knots used to attach a fly to the end of the tippet or the tippet to the ring on the end of a leader. The final tuck makes it a much more secure knot than the basic half blood knot. It works well for attaching a tippet to a ring, but is not as good as the Eugene bend for attaching a fly.

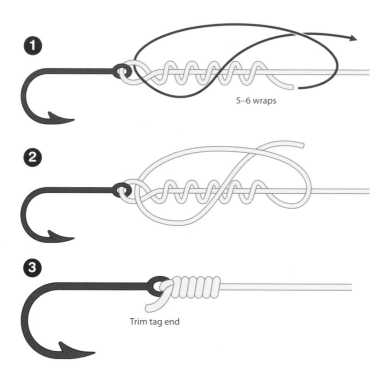

① 5–6 wraps

②

③ Trim tag end

1 Thread about 6 in (15 cm) of tippet through the eye of the hook, or the ring to which it is to be tied.
2 Keeping both parts of the line apart with your thumb and finger, wrap the tag end round the standing part five or six times.
3 Pass the tag end through the loop by the hook eye or ring.
4 Now pass the tag end through the loop that you have just formed. This is the tucked part of the knot.
5 Tighten the knot by moistening it and pulling on the standing part.
6 Finish the knot by trimming the tag end.

Right Spools of tippet material can become unwound all too easily. This device is an unusual and expensive answer to the problem – a tippet dispenser made by a Dutchman, Ari 't Hart

Tippets

In use a (short) leader of about 5 ft (1.5 m) in length will be extended by adding a tippet, which can be anything up to 5 ft (1.5 m) long itself, so doubling the length of the leader. A good length of leader is around 9 ft (2.75 m), or about the same length as your rod. If your leader is too short the end of your fly line will be too close to the fly, but a very long leader can be difficult to cast with, particularly on windy days when casting into the wind.

TIPPET MATERIAL

A range of strengths of tippet material will be required to match the size of fly being fished and the size of fish you are planning to catch. One reason why you will need a range of thicknesses/strengths of tippet material is because a strong, thick tippet will not go through the eye of a small hook. But to balance the size and bulk of a big fly, you will need a thicker tippet. You will also need thicker tippets for some stillwater leaders, as well as the leader itself. Some of the newer materials, such as copolymer, are very much thinner than nylon and can cause confusion as, in certain situations, you do not want a

tippet that is too thin. But for a given diameter of copolymer you can use a material that is very much stronger than nylon, or for a given strength you can use something much thinner. This can be a real advantage when fishing with small flies. You will also need some way of managing your various strengths of tippet material.

Which is the best tippet material to buy? Again there is a wide choice of materials and makes.

The basic tippet material is nylon, which has been around a very long time and its good and bad points are well known. It is soft, flexible and slightly stretchy so it will absorb hard pulls from a big fish, and it knots well. Then there is the just-mentioned copolymer, which was introduced in the 1980s. It is made using a process called copolymerization to combine two or more nylon monomers, which are extruded into a single strand. This offers high abrasion resistance and better knot strength than nylon, as well as low stretch and thin diameters.

Fluorocarbon, which was developed in Japan, has a similar refractive index to water, which makes it almost invisible in water. Fluorocarbon is denser than nylon, which means that it will sink faster. It is a polymer of fluorine that is bonded chemically with carbon to create a polymer that can be extruded. It has minimal water absorption, so knot strength is very good. A plus-point is that it does not degrade like nylon so you do not have to buy new spools every year. But if you drop any on the ground – which you should never do – it may be a hazard for wildlife.

Try to buy tippet material that is supplied on interlocking spools, as clipping two or three together makes a neat dispenser system. Make sure as well that you have an elastic band round each spool to hold the line in place and to keep the sun off. As with buying a rod, or line, don't buy anything too exotic to start with. Go for a well-respected brand of nylon monofilament.

Flies

While there are many hundreds of different patterns of dry flies, nymphs and stillwater flies, in each category there is a small number of must-have patterns that will catch fish almost anywhere in the world. (The actual patterns are illustrated in the relevant chapters.) You will need just a small range of flies to start with and it is often more important to have a range of different sizes of a small number of patterns, rather than lots of different patterns. Fishing the right size of fly for the conditions is often the key to success. Hooks are numbered to differentiate sizes, with the smallest hooks having the highest numbers: a size 22 hook is very much smaller than a size 12. So, make sure that you buy a range of sizes, for example hook sizes 14, 16 and 18 for dry flies and perhaps 12s, 14s and 16s for some of the nymph patterns. As well as buying flies in different sizes, always buy at least three of a pattern/size. The reason for this is that if you have a fly that is catching fish, it is all too easy to lose it or damage it beyond use (although there are times when a well-chewed fly will catch a lot of fish, so don't discard a fly just because it looks a bit bedraggled). If a lost or badly damaged fly was the only one of its type you had, that might bring your day to a premature end. Inevitably there will be times when you use and perhaps lose your last fly of a particular size or pattern, but by buying a number every time, you reduce the possibility. If you have a day when you lose a lot of flies, don't forget to buy replacements.

FLY BOXES

Although people have different ways of storing and managing their flies, to start with you will need one box for dry flies and another for nymphs and wet flies. Always try to keep the different types of fly in their own box. Fly boxes can be bought in different colours, which makes choosing the right box that much easier – as do transparent lids. They also have different ways of holding flies. Fly boxes with lots of small compartments, often with sprung lids, are good for keeping large bushy flies such as Grey Wulffs. A major drawback is that you run the risk of a gust of wind blowing the contents of an open compartment onto the ground or water. For regular use, boxes with ripple or slitted foam interiors are recommended.

tippet. They come in a wide range of shapes and styles, but choose a pair with straight cutting blades, rather than nail clippers with curved blades, and a built-in pin which you can use to undo knots and clean-out the eyes of hooks. Some have a recessed pin and others a retractable one.

FORCEPS OR HAEMOSTATS

A pair of forceps, or haemostats, can be used to unhook fish in the water, remove a fly from a fish's mouth and crush the barb on a hook when you want or need to fish with barbless or de-barbed hooks.

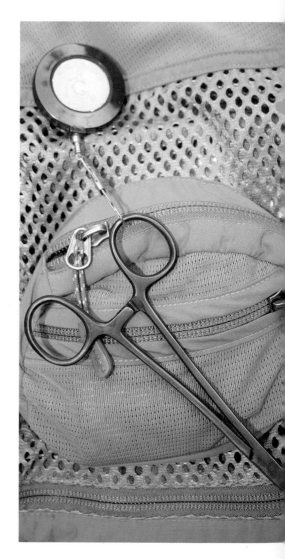

Choose fly boxes that will display your flies well and hold them securely – so that they will not fall out or get blown away by the wind

They do a very good job of holding the flies in place securely as well as allowing their easy removal when required. Slitted foam holds flies by the bend of the hook, which is pushed into the slit. They also hold flies so that the hackles do not get squashed or flattened. Never buy a box that holds the flies under metal clips as these will flatten hackles and can start hooks rusting.

There are also fly boxes fitted with what are known as threaders. These are small loops of very fine wire that are a great aid to threading a tippet through the eye of a fly. The threader is poked through the eye of the hook and the tippet passed through the threader loop, which is then used to draw the tippet back through the eye. This is a big help for those with less than perfect eyesight, or for changing flies in poor light.

Right Pin-on reels can be bought with lines of different lengths, depending on the intended use. When using a pair of forceps to unhook a fish, you will need a long line so that you can reach the fish in the water

Other necessary equipment

LEADER CLIPPERS

A good pair of leader clippers is essential, as you will need them every time you change your fly or

Leader clippers are a quick and easy way to cut leaders and tippets. They can't get in a tangle like a pair of scissors or stuck in a waistcoat pocket

FLY AND LEADER FLOATANT

Paste-type or gel floatants that melt with the heat from your fingers are the best, as you can apply the floatant to the whole fly or just specific parts. You cannot do this with a bottle of liquid floatant into which you dunk your fly. Some are sold in little tubs and others in small plastic bottles. The bottles can be attached to your vest with a bottom-up floatant holder. Beware that on a very hot day the floatant will be liquid and can go everywhere when you take the cap off the bottle. A little pot, or tub, of floatant paste is essential for greasing your leader to ensure that it stays afloat, particularly when fishing nymphs.

BOTTOM-UP FLOATANT HOLDER

A bottom-up floatant holder is a soft plastic cup into which you push the bottom of your bottle of floatant and then clip it onto your waistcoat or chest pack in a convenient position. There are also versions made in leather and some with elastic straps to hold the bottle.

Fly and leader floatants are used to help your fly and leader stay afloat. Apply floatant to a fly very sparingly. If you coat a fly thickly it will not float better or longer. It will probably sink quicker

A bottom-up floatant holder keeps your fly floatant in a handy position, ready for action

PIN-ON REELS, OR RETRACTORS

Pin-on reels, or retractors, are a vital means of attaching small items of equipment to a waistcoat or chest pack. They have an extending line or sometimes a curly plastic line, with a clip on one end to which you attach your leader clippers, forceps or anything else. There are heavy-duty models, with long lines, which can be used with landing nets (see image on page 32).

BITE INDICATORS

Bite, take or strike indicators are used when fishing nymphs as they make more obvious any movement of your fly underwater or movement of the leader caused by a trout taking your nymph. However not everyone likes them. Some of them are so big that they are, in effect, a float that controls the depth at which your fly swims in the water. That is float fishing, not fly-fishing. But a small, discreet indicator gives the newcomer to nymph fishing something to concentrate on. Such indicators include strike putty, strike yarn and Kahuna LT strike indicators. Most of these indicators are available in different fluorescent colours (pink, orange, green, yellow) to suit different water and light conditions. Anglers with limited vision or difficulty seeing a dry fly – particularly small ones – on the water in certain light conditions may find the use of a discreet indicator helpful.

A bite indicator is an important visual aid for the newcomer to nymph fishing as it will alert you to a fish taking your fly. Shown here are: a length of orange Kahuna, some green strike indicator yarn, and a pink pinch-on foam indicator. The big Fish Pimp indicator will act as a float.

Strike putty is, as the name suggests, a mould-able putty that sticks to the leader. A tiny piece can be moulded round a knot on the leader to keep it in place. It will need renewing every now and then. If there is a ripple on the water surface it is not always the easiest to see. It can be bought in little tubs either as a single colour or two or four colours in one tub. Yarn indicators are more visible on windy days but they have the disadvantage that fish will rise to them, mistaking the indicator for a fly. In use a short length of yarn is tied round the leader and then trimmed to length. Kahuna LT strike indicators are made from fluorescent orange tube, very similar to a fly line, which you can cut to the length you require. The end of your leader is threaded through the piece of tubing, which can be left on permanently. The indicator is slim enough to pass through the rod rings – as will a small yarn indicator – but strike putty will come off as it goes through a ring.

LANDING NET

A landing net is used to net or land a fish and they come in all shapes, styles and sizes and are made from exotic hardwoods or aluminium tube. Wooden tennis-racket-style nets are very popular but as they have short handles, they are useless if you fish from a high bank. They are at their best when wading in a river, when a fish can be brought close to the angler so that it can be netted. Much more practical is a net with a longer handle, possibly telescopic, that will reach to the water. Folding nets are a mixed blessing. When folded they take up little space and don't get in the way too much but they can fail to open at the crucial moment. A net with a fixed frame over-comes this problem and has the added benefit that you can push the net into weeds to 'dig out' a fish that has taken refuge in a clump of weed. Knotted nets are not allowed as they can damage a fish's skin, and some of the latest nets are of soft synthetic rubber – these are the kindest to fish.

Stillwater anglers will need a landing net with a much longer handle than is ever likely to be needed on a river. The handle can be either fixed or telescopic. The reason for needing a long

Tennis-racket-style nets are very popular but they have their limitations. To net a fish with one you have to get it very close to you because of the short handle which can put too much strain on your rod. This model is fitted with a special soft net to minimize damage to a fish when netting it

Nets with fixed frames are fail-safe as there is no folded frame to refuse to open

Tim Gaunt-Baker

Unless you have your net attached to you it is all too easy to drop it or put it down and walk off without it

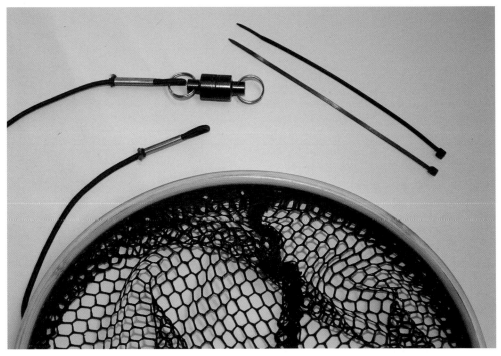

A two-piece magnetic net holder can be fixed to the frame of a net with cable ties

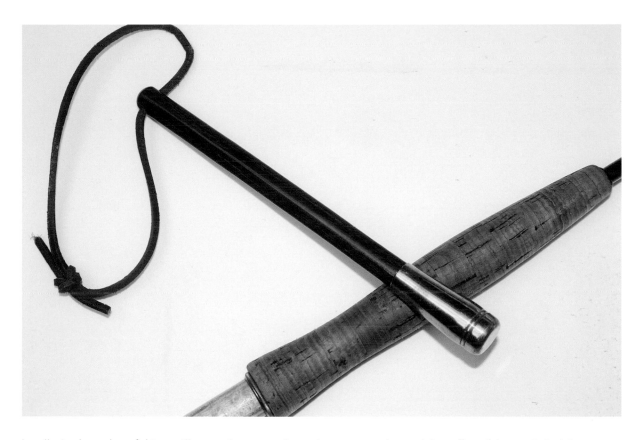

A priest is the most efficient and humane instrument to use to kill a fish

handle is that when fishing stillwaters long leaders and more than one fly are often used and it can be difficult if not impossible to wind-in enough line and leader to reach a fish in the water with a net with only a short handle (see Chapter 9).

Before buying a net, a major consideration is how you are going to carry it. You need to be able to it attach it to your person so that you cannot put it down and leave it on the bank, but it should be easily accessible when needed.

While you can buy a scabbard with a belt loop to hold a folding net, hanging a net from the loop on the back of a waistcoat is best. If you have a net with a long handle and the end of that handle is uppermost, the net bag will be near the ground and will get caught on bushes and brambles. Attaching the net the other way up, with the net uppermost, will overcome this problem. It will also mean that when you reach behind you to grasp your net, you will get hold of the handle rather than the net, and because the weight of

the net is uppermost, the pendulum effect of the hanging net will be much less. A two-piece magnetic net holder is a good device to consider and they are available in models which can be attached to the net hoop, or the end of the handle.

A good way to attach a magnetic net holder to your net is with one or two plastic cable ties. The lanyard must be attached to the end of the handle otherwise it will get in the way when trying to use your net. A net retractor is also worth considering, but they can be fixed only to the handle.

PRIEST

A priest is used for administering the last rites – killing – any fish you want to take home to eat. It can also be used to kill an injured or sick fish, if the rules allow.

If you are fishing water where the rule is 'no kill' then you cannot put an injured fish out of its misery: it must be returned to the water alive.

Polarized glasses reduce the surface glare from the water, helping you to see into the water as well as providing essential protection for your eyes

Never try to kill a fish with a stone, piece of wood or landing net handle – they are not designed for the job. To kill a fish, hold it firmly (ideally still in your landing net) and apply two or three sharp blows with your priest to the back of the fish's head. Make sure that you keep your fingers clear of the target area.

Priests can be made from staghorn and different woods and metals in varying combinations: they will all do the same job.

POLARIZED GLASSES

Polarized glasses are a must for two very good reasons. First they will protect your eyes from an errant fly on the end of your line if, for example, it is blown back into your face on a windy day. Second they allow you to see into the water. Glasses designed for fishing are available in a wide range of styles – some with side pieces which stop extraneous light from getting into your eyes – and with different coloured lenses. In general brown, copper or vermillion lenses are the best for all-round use. Grey lenses are all

right but not exceptional, while yellow cannot be recommended as they are only any use in low light conditions. In low light conditions, such as at dusk or on grey, gloomy days, you may be able to see better if you take your glasses off. If you do, remember that your eyes will be unprotected.

Prescription fishing sunglasses, with polarized lenses, are available, as are clip-ons for those who wear glasses. Don't forget to buy a retaining cord or string so that you can take off your glasses and not have to put them in a pocket or on the ground and probably walk off without them or even tread on them.

TORCH

A small torch is not essential but it can be useful, particularly when changing flies in failing light or even finding your way back to your car in the dark. When using a torch on the riverbank, stand with your back to the water so that fish are not frightened by the light. It is possible to buy a pin-on reel with a built-in LED light.

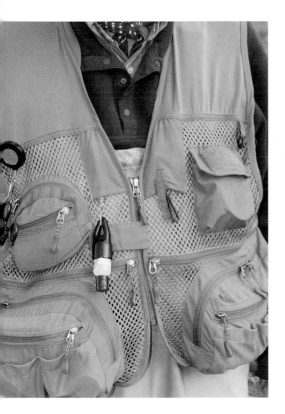

more durable than a zip as well as being cooler in hot weather. As you don't wear a waistcoat to keep warm and it is often more difficult to stay cool on a hot day, there is much to be said for buying a mesh vest, which provides good ventilation. If you are fishing on a chilly day you can always wear an extra sweater or fleece.

As a confirmed advocate of waistcoats, I am not the best person to promote the benefits of the various waist and chest packs that are available. They have their supporters and some of the smaller versions would seem to fill the gap between the minimalist/lanyard approach and the full-on multi-pocket fly vest. Whichever you go for, choose a design that is comfortable, efficient and has adequate carrying capacity.

A chest pack holds all the angler's accessories compactly and is easily accessible

While waistcoats, or vests, may be losing some popularity to chest packs, they are still a very good way to organize and carry your tackle and accessories

WAISTCOAT OR CHEST PACK

You will need something to carry everything in an orderly and easily accessible way. Although traditional fishing bags are still made, they are inefficient and uncomfortable to carry, as the weight of the bag rests on one shoulder only and there is no way to keep all your tackle in an orderly fashion. They are best avoided.

For short visits to a river or lake, a minimalist approach is to take a few spools of tippet material, clippers, floatant and two small boxes of flies, all of which can be carried in the pockets of a fishing shirt and attached to a lanyard which you wear round your neck.

A waistcoat should have pockets where you want them and pockets that will hold, for example, your fly boxes. Waistcoats can be held together at the front by either a webbing strap and clip, or a zip. The clip system is stronger and

A handmade leather chest pack with pockets to hold a pair of forceps and fly floatant on the wearer's right-hand side. On the left is another way of carrying a number of spools of tippet material

FOOTWEAR AND CLOTHING

Try to wear comfortable and practical clothing that blends with your surroundings. White or very pale shirts are out, as are white sun hats. A hat, or cap, can help you see into the river better as its peak will shield your eyes from the sun as well as keeping your head warm on a cold day or preventing sunburn on a sunny day. Carry a light-weight waterproof jacket in the back pocket of your waistcoat for days when the weather is changeable or it might rain.

Suitable footwear includes a pair of gumboots, walking boots if you know every-thing underfoot is going to be dry, through to wading boots worn with either waist or chest waders. Although it is possible to buy inexpen-sive nylon waders, they will quickly become unwearable in warm weather because they do not breathe. As a result of internal condensation on a hot day your clothes can be almost as wet

as if you were not wearing waders. There is a very simple answer to the problem: breathable waders. Breathable waders have revolutionized life for anglers. Even in hot conditions you can wade the river, walk the banks, sit around and do anything else during a day's fishing without getting hot and sweaty or finding that your clothes are wet when you get out of your waders at the end of the day. Bliss! Chest waders can have a front zip which makes them easier to get into and take off, as well easing access if you need a pee. Waders keep your legs dry if river banks are covered in high and wet vegetation, or if it starts raining. For anyone who does not need, or indeed want, to wade too deep, waist waders are worth considering. They will allow deeper wading than traditional thigh boots but obviously not as deep as chest waders – and they will keep your bottom dry if you sit on a wet bank or seat. Readers planning to fish small

stillwaters are unlikely to need chest waders as many such fisheries either have a complete ban on wading or allow the use of thigh waders only. In such circumstances, gumboots and a pair of waterproof over-trousers will keep you dry on a wet day.

Breathable waders were very expensive but can now be bought for very reasonable sums of money. Waist-high or chest waders come with what are known as boot feet – built-in boots – or with stocking feet (neoprene socks). Stocking foot waders can only be worn with a pair of wading boots. They should have built-in gravel guards, made from neoprene or wader fabric, which go over the ankles of your wading boots to stop grit, sand and small stones from getting into your boots. Whichever type of waders you buy, make sure that the waders themselves, if boot foot, or the wading boots have rubber soles, preferably studded.

Avoid buying anything with felt soles as they are losing favour very rapidly because they can harbour infections and pernicious microorganisms which can survive for quite long periods in the soles, particularly if they are damp and not allowed to dry thoroughly. (Drying felt soles thoroughly or spraying them with a suitable disinfectant can kill these nasty organisms and help prevent their spread from river to river.) The rubber soles on wading boots are very different from those on gumboots as the rubber material used has benefited from rock-climbing technology which developed 'sticky' rubber. Coupled with studs, these soles will provide first-class grip and traction on rocky riverbeds and, when fishing from grassy riverbanks, they will not slip like felt soles can. Felt soles and wet grass on a sloping river bank are a potentially lethal combination.

Wading boots with studded rubber soles will provide good grip on most surfaces likely to be encountered by an angler. Rubber soles have the added benefit of being less likely to harbour infectious organisms

CHAPTER THREE

Putting your tackle together

This chapter tells you how to put together your newly acquired tackle at home so that everything is ready for action, and how to assemble it all before starting fishing. At this stage there is nothing to do with your fly rod apart from admire it.

The reel and line

The first thing to do when you take your fly reel out of the box is to make sure that you can wind-in line with your chosen hand. Most reels are convertible for left-hand or right-hand wind and instructions how to do this will be supplied in the box. But which hand do you choose? If you are right-handed and want to wind your reel with your right hand, when you wind-in line you will have to hold your rod in your left hand. While this may seem to be a disadvantage, it does mean that when you are casting, the reel handle will be out of the way and so the line cannot get wrapped around it. This is an important consideration. If you are left-handed, then the reverse is the case. But if you are right-handed and have your reel set up to wind with your left hand, then there is no need to change hands, although you may have the problem of your line getting caught round the reel handle.

Before you can put your fly line on your reel you have to put on some backing. Although tackle shops and online suppliers will fit backing and a fly line to a reel when you buy all three – you can also buy pre-loaded reels – it is helpful to know how to do it yourself if, for example, you buy another spool for your reel or you want to change line.

Most reel-makers advise backing capacities for their reels. For example a reel will accommodate 75 m of standard 22 lb (10 kg) braided polyester, 100 m of 20 lb (9 kg) micro-backing and 250 m of 25lb (11.4 kg) gel-spun polyethylene (generally used only for saltwater fly fishing when a lot of backing can be required). This means that you can buy a specific length of backing and be reasonably confident that it and the line will fill the reel spool. If you have no idea how much backing a reel will take, the only way to find out is to fit the fly line first and then the backing. It's tedious, fiddly and can result in a tangled and knotted line. But if you have a spare or second spool, you can wind the fly line onto it, followed by enough backing to fill the spool. Now you can attach the end of the backing to the other spool and transfer the backing and

Modern fly reels are usually easy to convert from left-hand to right-hand wind, or vice versa. Here a retaining clip is removed so that a one-way bearing, in the centre of the reel, can be extracted and turned over before refitting it

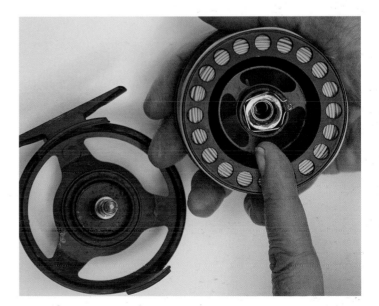

A fly reel with backing installed, ready to be attached to the end of the fly line

line to it. The process is explained shortly. You can also make a reasonable estimate by comparing the reel with one of a similar size and known capacity and use that figure. Most reels are fitted with quick-release spools, with usually a little sliding lever or tab to release the spool.

When the spool is filled correctly the line will be just below the rim of the spool. If you over-fill the spool you run the risk of the reel jamming because, as you wind line back onto the reel when fishing, it won't go back on as evenly and firmly as when you first wound-on the line. An over-full spool can jam the line against the reel cage.

Pushing the slider will release the spool. Some reels have a little lever instead

A spool that is filled correctly will have the maximum length of backing under the fly line but not so much that the line may get jammed

ATTACHING THE BACKING

When you know how much backing to use:
1 Attach the end of the backing line to the spool using an arbor knot. To tie this knot, pass the end of the backing round the spool, between the spool and the foot of the reel, and tie an overhand knot round the line.
2 Next, tie a second overhand, or thumb knot, in the tag end of the line. Tighten that knot and trim off any excess line. Now tighten the line and the first knot against the reel arbor. The second knot acts as a stopper knot.
3 Before winding the backing onto your reel spool, make sure that it winds onto the *bottom* of the spool.
4 Pass a pencil or similar object through the spool of backing line so that you can sit down and hold the spool between your knees and it can revolve smoothly. If you lay the spool flat on the floor, the backing will twist and may become tangled.
5 Hold the reel in one hand and the backing with your thumb and fingers, applying tension as you wind it evenly, from side to side, onto the spool.

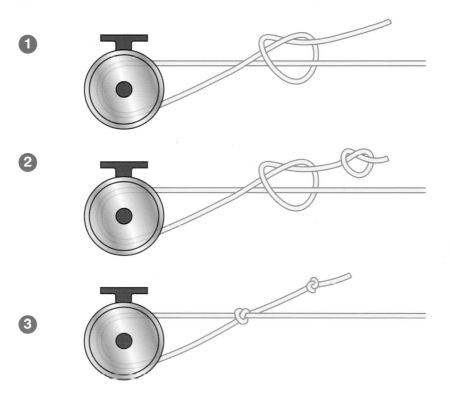

Do as the label says!

ATTACHING THE FLY LINE TO THE BACKING

Once all the backing is on the reel, you must attach the fly line to the backing. Make sure that you use the correct end of a weight-forward line, which will be identified with a label saying 'Attach this end to spool' or words to that effect. The best way to make the attachment is with a tube nail knot.

Although this knot is often called a nail knot, it is much easier to tie using a piece of small diameter tube instead of a nail. A piece of clean ballpoint pen ink tube is ideal. Once again, make sure that you attach the backing to the end of the line marked 'This end to reel'.

TYING A TUBE NAIL KNOT

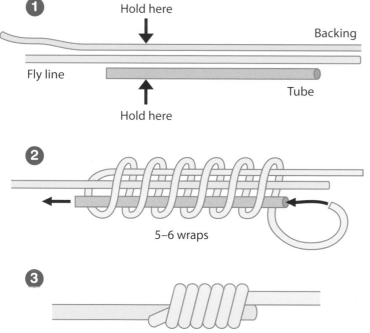

1 Hold the tube and the end of the fly line, together, with your left thumb and forefinger, with the end of the fly line pointing to the right (if you are right-handed). Hold the backing with the end pointing to the left.
2 Wrap the end of the backing around the fly line and tube five or six times. Keep the turns as close together as possible and hold them with your thumb and finger.
3 Pull on the tag end of the backing to tighten the coils. Now insert the end of the backing through the tube.
4 Remove the tube (ensuring that the tag end of the backing is still accessible) and pull on both ends of the backing to tighten the knot, ensuring that the coils lie close together. Don't let the loops formed at each end of the tube slide under the wraps.
5 Finish the knot by trimming the tag end of both backing and fly line. Test the knot by pulling firmly on both backing and line.

Another way to attach the backing to the reel-end of your fly line is by fitting a braided loop to the line. Many fly lines are supplied with a braided loop in the box. Handle the braided loop carefully as it is very easy to find that it has started to unravel and there is not a long enough length of braid into which to insert the end of the line. You fit the braided loop by sliding the end of the line into the tube and then working the braid along the line until it won't go any further. Thread a short length of monofilament through the loop and then through the length of tube supplied with the loop. Slide the tube over the eye of the loop and over the braid on the line. For extra security you can apply a drop of superglue to the braid before fitting the tubing. Trim any untidy ends of the braid before sliding the tube so that it covers the ends of the braid.

With your fly line now attached firmly to the backing on the reel spool, put a suitable axle through the hole in the middle of the fly line and its spool, as you did with the backing, and then wind the line onto the spool. Keep some tension on the line as you do this and move the line from side to side so that the line lies flat and even on the spool or arbor.

Some fly lines are sold with a self-adhesive printed sticker which you can put on the spool to remind you what line is on the reel. If you have one, apply it to the back of the spool where it will be protected.

WHEN YOU DON'T KNOW HOW MUCH BACKING TO USE

When you don't know how much backing to use, the process is similar but in reverse as you wind on the fly line first, followed by backing. Before you do this, join the backing to the end of the fly line, using the tube nail knot as described above. Then:

1 Attach the end of the fly line to the reel arbor with a simple knot and hold the line while you wind on enough turns for the line to grip the spool.
2 Wind on all the line and then the backing. You have put on enough backing when the backing is about ¼ in (6 mm) from the top edge of the spool. Do not fill the spool completely. Cut the backing to length if necessary.
3 Now remove the backing and then the fly line. Coil the backing and then line in large loops around the back of a chair or a cardboard box to prevent them getting tangled.
4 Attach the free end of the backing to the spool, as above, and then wind-on as above. If everything goes smoothly, you will end up with the spool filled to the correct level and the right end of the fly line exposed ready to be attached to a leader.

Fitting a braided loop to the end of a fly line can be a fiddly process but once done it produces a neat loop

When making a loop-to-loop connection it is important to pass the right piece of line through the right loop

HOW TO MAKE A LOOP IN THE END OF A FLY LINE

There are various ways to connect your fly line to the leader but the easiest and most practical is to have a loop on the end of the line and leader so that you can use the loop-to-loop connection. But to be able to use that method, you do need a loop on the end of your fly line. Some manufacturers finish their lines with a factory-made loop on the business end. The braided loop that you may have

If you buy a fly line with a factory-made loop on the front end, you do not need to worry about how to attach a leader to it

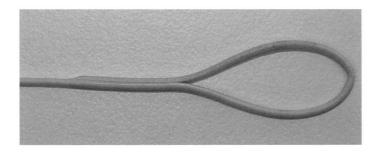

Right A loop made on the end of your line, using the line itself, is better than fitting a braided loop as it will not absorb water

fitted to the reel-end of your line is not the best way to add a loop to the business-end of your line. You can however make a very efficient loop quite easily with some waterproof superglue and a short length of silicone tube. (Suitable glue and tubing can be bought from fishing tackle shops. Try coarse fishing or carp supply shops for silicone tubing.)

1 Start by making a small loop, of about ½ in (12.5 mm) diameter with about 1½ in (38 mm) of the end of the line.
2 Hold the loop and apply a small drop of super-glue to the two pieces of line, which must be lying parallel to each other.
3 When the glue has set, apply a little run of glue to both sides of the line and hold while it cures.
4 Finish the loop by covering the glued part with a length of silicone tube that is just longer than the glued area of fly line. To slide the tube over the loop and join, take a short length of thick monofilament fishing line, or tippet material (it wants to be thick so that it will not cut the fly line), and pass it through the loop.
5 Take both ends of the mono and thread through the silicone tube and then slide the tube over the loop and onto the glued section so that the tube finishes on the line.

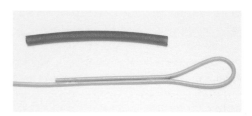

Covering the join with the silicone tube helps the end of the fly line to pass smoothly through the top ring on your rod.

SETTING THE DRAG ON YOUR REEL

Another important operation is to set the drag on your reel. Apart from very simple inexpensive fly reels, most reels have some form of adjustable drag. Basic reels have a non-adjustable click drag to prevent the spool from revolving too quickly when you strip-off line (if the spool does spin too fast you risk getting your line in a tangle, usually referred to as a bird's nest). A poorly designed system that does not operate smoothly and consistently will be a menace, as it is very likely to apply too much tension to your line just as a fish makes a rush for freedom, perhaps breaking your tippet at a crucial moment.

A good drag prevents the reel back-spooling, or over-runs, and feeds out line smoothly. It is important to set it correctly. This is done most easily when you have a line on your reel. It is better to err on the light side (and do resist the temptation to tighten the drag while you are playing a strong fish). There is a good way to start setting the drag on a reel by holding the reel in one hand and the end of the line in the other. The hand holding the line adjusts the drag knob so that when you let go of the reel, it will descend slowly to the floor. If the drag is not tight enough it will hit the floor; when it is just right, the reel will descend slowly, land lightly on the floor and stay standing on its rim. As you will hold the line in your hand nearly all the time when playing a fish, you want the drag set to stop over-runs. To check this, once again hold the reel in one hand and the end of the line in the other. Now give the line a jerk, which should make the reel turn and line come off the spool easily but not to excess. You can check whether the drag is set correctly by holding your arms out in front of you and moving your hands apart as quickly as possible. If the line between your hands is straight, then the drag is set too tight and if there is a long loop of line, then it is not quite tight enough. The ideal is when the line hangs in a shallow curve.

ATTACHING THE LEADER

Once you have put all the line on your reel and adjusted the drag setting, if necessary, you can attach a leader, using the loop-to-loop connection. There is no need to worry about adding a tippet length at this stage. You can do this when you are ready to start fishing.

MAKING A LOOP TO LOOP CONNECTION

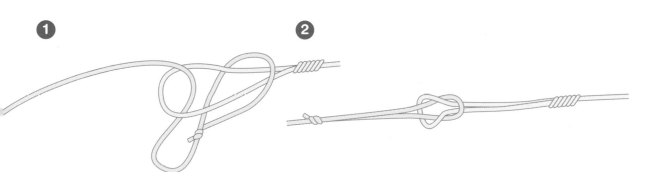

1   Pass the loop on the end of the line to be added over the end of the line to which you are adding a new length of line.
2   Now pass the end of the line being added through the loop on the end of the other line.

3   Pull it all the way through so that the loops come together.
4   Done correctly, the two loops should interlock to form a square knot.

Organizing your tackle and accessories

Organizing and deciding where to store all your items of tackle and accessories in a waistcoat is an interesting and seemingly endless challenge. But to begin at the end, once you are happy with where everything is – stick with it. If you can reach for things automatically and without thinking, it can save you valuable time if you need to make a quick change of fly before a hatch comes to an end or it is too dark to see what you are doing. And always make sure that you close a pocket after use as it is easy for a fly box, for example, to slip out and be lost.

If you follow the basic principle of having everything that you are most likely to need and use most often in easily accessible pockets, you won't go far wrong. Fly boxes should go in outside front pockets. Spools of tippet material can be kept in a small front pocket, perhaps one of the higher ones. Your leader clipper is something that will be used every time you change a fly or tie a knot in a length of mono. It is best attached permanently to the front of your waistcoat with a pin-on reel, or zinger, so that it is always easily accessible and you cannot drop it or put it down and lose it. Fishing glasses can be kept in a case in

an inside pocket, or a long vertical pocket, as they will be taken out of their case at the start of the day and most probably not returned to it until the end of the day. If you need glasses to change flies and you have not got prescription sunglasses, find an easily and quickly accessible pocket for them. A priest is something else best kept in a long pocket.

A bottom-up holder for gel-type fly floatant (see photo on page 33) can be fixed to the front of your waistcoat so that it is easily accessible when you want to apply floatant to a fly. Floatant that is used to grease a leader can be kept in a less-accessible place, as it is something that will not be used that often during a day's fishing. A pin-on reel with a long line will be needed for a pair of forceps so that you can reach into a fish to remove your fly from its mouth. Position the pin-on reel so that the forceps hang out of the way but can still be found easily when needed.

If your waistcoat has a back pocket, that is a good place to store a lightweight wading jacket or waterproof ready for a shower of rain. Waistcoats are usually equipped with a D-ring on the back of the neck from which to hang your landing net. The simplest way to attach a landing net to the D-ring is with a spring clip, similar to those

Once you have taken your rod out of its tube and bag and assembled it, you will need to put it somewhere safe so that it does not get damaged or even broken

used on dog leads. However, in order to use your landing net you will have to reach round and unhook the clip: simple but not very efficient. It is much better to have your net attached permanently to your waistcoat with an elastic, shock-cord lanyard so that you can reach out to net a fish – then you can't lose the net if you put it down and then forget to pick it up. You can get magnetic net holders (see photo on page 36) which have two halves that snap together. Pulling the handle of the net will break the magnet's grip so that you can use it and, after use, holding the half of the magnet fixed to the net close to the half on your waistcoat will return the net to its safe stowage. An alternative is a special heavy-duty pin-on reel with a long Kevlar or Spectra line.

Assembling your tackle ready for action

Fly rods are very strong and surprisingly robust when used for their designed purpose: casting a fly and playing fish. But they are fragile when someone stands on a rod or if you shut the tip in the car door. Shutting a rod in a car door is a major reason for rods getting broken. If that should happen and you have not got a spare rod available, it will mean the end of the day before it has

even started. Start a good habit by putting your rod together last. If your rod has a protective tube and a rod bag, or just a rod bag, take the sections out of the bag and put them somewhere safe (what constitutes safe is discussed shortly), and then put the tube and/or bag to one side or back in your car.

ASSEMBLING THE ROD AND REEL

Assembling a three- or four-piece rod is best done by fitting the reel to the bottom, or butt, section first. This means that you have just a short section of rod to deal with, rather than manoeuvring the complete rod about. When you fit the reel to the reel seat, make sure that the reel handle is on the correct side. Turn your rod so that the fly keeper ring (on a multi-piece rod – see later this section) or guides (on a two-piece rod) are uppermost. With the reel in the seat, the handle will be on the opposite side (but it will be right when you turn the rod so the reel is under the handle). One end of the reel foot will slide under a fixed hood and the other will be held by a sliding band, or hood, which is locked in place by a knurled-screw locking ring. Do not over-tighten this ring by using pliers or anything similar: solid finger tension is all that is needed. (It pays to check every

As well as fitting the reel so that the handle is on the right side, you need to make sure that it will line up with the bottom ring, or guide, on the butt section of your rod

Although alignment dots help you to assemble a rod correctly, it is always a good idea to check the alignment by sighting through the guides or along the back of the rod

Always use the end of the fly line, not the leader or tippet, when threading the line through the rod rings or guides

now and then that the reel is still tight during a day on the water.) Now attach the next section – the next thickest – which you should hold close to the ferrule. When joining two sections together, make sure that one is about twenty-five degrees out of alignment with the other so that you can twist the sections into alignment, tightening them at the same time. Then join together the top sections and finish by attaching them to the bottom two sections. Some rods have a little white dot by the ferrule to help alignment as you join each piece, but do check that the rod rings, or guides, are in line by sighting along the rod and through the rings.

Adjustments can be made by twisting the errant section slightly before making sure that the sections are pushed together firmly, with a slight twist as before. With a two-piece rod simply fit the two sections together, check they are aligned and then tighten the join. Don't forget to check that the reel is aligned correctly with the rod guides.

THREADING THE LINE

Once your rod and reel are assembled, you will need to thread the leader and line through the guides. Instead of trying to thread the fine, near-

invisible end of the leader or tippet through the rings, take the end of the fly line and thread that.

It is so much easier – and quicker – when you can see what you are working with. Also, making a loop in the end of the fly line will stop it slipping back through the guides if you let go of the line by mistake. Pull about 10–12 ft (3–3.65 m) of line from the reel with one hand while holding the rod with the other, so that you have slack line to work with. Make sure that you thread the line/leader through every guide and that you don't wrap the line around the rod by mistake. It's very easy to make both mistakes, particularly when you are in a hurry to get started! The first and biggest guide, or stripping guide, will be around 2 ft (60 cm) above the top of the handle. To thread the line through the guides near the top-end of the rod, place the rod butt on some grass if possible – try to avoid mud, sand or tarmac – angle the rod over and take a pace or two towards the tip, threading the line as you go. Don't bend the top of the rod in an effort to reach the top ring.

When you have threaded the line and leader through all the rings, hold the end of the leader in your rod hand and wind in any slack line. If you let go of the leader, it and the line will slip back through the guides and you will have to thread it all again. If you thread the line and leader after you have got everything else ready, and have put on your waders (if wearing waders) and waistcoat, you can keep hold of the end of the leader with the hand with which you are holding your rod. This will prevent it from falling back through the guides as you won't have to put your rod down or need to let go of the end of the fly line.

At some stage of getting ready to go fishing, on the riverbank or back at your car at the end of the day, you will want to put your rod down. Never lay it on the ground, as someone can stand on it or even drive over it in a car. Always lean it standing up where it can be seen. There may be a

tree or bush handy, or a car door mirror can be a good support. If you have an estate car, or hatchback, most rods can be passed through the back door and laid over the back of the seats with the rod tip by the windscreen. Another option is a magnetic rod holder that you stick on the side of the car and place your rod in to stop it from being blown over. Don't forget to put it back in the car after you taken your rod out.

Fly rods are fitted with a little ring (usually fixed, sometimes folding) just above the rod handle, known as a fly keeper ring. The idea is that you hook your fly in the ring and then reel-in your line, keeping everything neat and tidy while you move along the riverbank or to the next casting place on a stillwater. Do yourself a favour and forget that it is there (other than using it to line up your reel). There is a very much better way. Although using the fly keeper ring does keep things tidy, it has one major failing. And that is, when your leader is longer than the length of your rod, the leader-line join will be between the top ring and the reel, with no fly line outside the top guide. This makes it difficult to start casting after you have unhooked your fly, as you will have to pull the leader through the guides until there is some line the action-side of the top ring. Instead, make sure that you have some slack line outside the top ring and then hook your fly into the highest ring next to the top ring. Put your

Hooking your fly into the rod guide nearest the tip when moving along the river bank and not casting. Never hook your fly into the cork of the rod handle as doing this repeatedly will result in damage to the handle

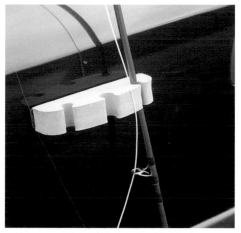

Shutting the tip of a rod in a car door is one of the most common ways of breaking a rod. A magnetic rod holder is a very good way of keeping it safe when you are not holding it

A tippet is a sacrificial length of monofilament. Pull a length about a yard, or a metre, from a spool of the breaking strain that you want to use

fingers through the resulting loop in the line and pull It down to the reel and then place it round the spool. Hold the loop around the spool and reel-up any slack. With an average length leader you will have some line outside the top ring, which makes it much easier to start casting when you unloop the line from around the reel and then unhook your fly.

ATTACHING THE TIPPET

If you have attached your leader to the end of your fly line using a loop-to-loop connection, then the only knot that you need now is the tucked half blood knot (see page 30 or page 172), which you can use to tie a tippet to the ring on the end of your leader.

Before attaching the tippet, wait until you are

Fishing a stream as small as this requires careful and accurate casting and even more so on windy days when a bad cast could end up with your fly in the bankside vegetation

A neoprene pouch is a good way to protect a reel from scratches and other damage

ready to start fishing and know what pattern and size of fly you will be using so you can match the correct strength/thickness of tippet to the fly.

Packing up at the end of the day

When you finish a day's fishing you will have to take your tackle apart and put everything away. If you want to, you can cut your fly off the end of the tippet, on the riverbank, and return it to the right fly box (always make sure that you never leave any monofilament in the hook eye), and then reel-in all the fly line and leader ready to walk back to your car. If you decide to leave your fly on the end of the line, hooked into the top guide then, at the car, the first thing to do is to remove your fly and reel-in the line. Remove the reel, while leaning your rod somewhere safe, and put it back in its pouch, if you have got one.

Now you can start to dismantle your rod. Pull the sections apart with a firm, straight pull and try not to bend the rod. Next, put each section back into the rod bag, thick end first for all sections except the handle, which will then help to protect the thin top section, and put the bag in the rod tube (if you have one). Once the expensive and easily damaged items have been dealt with, unhook your landing net (you may want to do this first if it is getting in the way) and put it in the back of the car safely. Polarized glasses can be returned to their case and, along with your waistcoat, also put in the car. Finally, change out of your waders, wading boots, or gumboots. And, before driving off, have a good look round to make sure that you have not left anything on the ground.

Now that you have put all your tackle together and know how to assemble your rod and thread the line through the rod guides (and put everything away at the end of the day), it is time to find out how to get your fly to the fish that you want to catch.

CHAPTER FOUR

How to get your fly to the fish

Casting is the process of getting your fly to a fish that you want to catch. And until you can get your fly onto, or into, the water you cannot expect to catch fish. Being able to cast well is fundamental to successful fly fishing.

Until you can get your fly to a fish in the water, whether it is a river or stillwater, you cannot expect to catch. It can happen that you drop your fly on the water and a fish will rise and take it, but that is a rare occurrence and is not a technique to be relied on. An ability to cast is a fundamental requirement of fly fishing. Some fly fishermen maintain that you cannot learn to cast from a book: if that is true, then why do so many well-known casters write books on the subject? A book can give you a lot of background information and understanding of the principles involved in getting your fly to the fish. Such a basic understanding will help you get more out of any casting instruction that you decide to have. And yes, having some lessons with a qualified casting instructor will be money well spent. A good instructor will get you into good habits and stop you picking up bad ones.

Casting, in simple terms, is the process of getting your fly from where you are standing on the bank to a (feeding) fish in a river or stillwater, using your fly rod and fly line. But there is one problem. Try the simple experiment of throwing a feather and a small stone. However hard you try to throw the feather, it will not go far. The stone, by contrast, will go quite a long way because it has weight. A trout fly – with some exceptions – has virtually no weight (and big, heavy flies can actually be difficult to cast). The necessary weight has to be found somewhere. Coarse fishermen, or anyone who has watched a coarse angler casting, will know that the baited hook, split shot and a float combined together produce enough weight for the bait to be cast quite some distance. Now we have established that we need weight if we are going to cast our fly a worthwhile distance, what supplies the weight? The answer is a fly line. That is the reason why fly lines are thick. But a fly line is not simply a long, thick line. A fly line is a very sophisticated computer-designed, tapered

The end result of a successful cast should be a fish on the end of your line

length of synthetic materials. As we found out earlier, fly lines come in different weights for different weights of fly rod, in different tapers, and designed either to float or to sink at a range of different speeds and to different depths. The line rating number is based on the weight of the first 30 ft (9.1 m) of fly line beyond the rod tip, and that weight/length of line will allow the rod to perform to its optimum.

There are two basic casts, the first of which is the overhead cast. This cast consists of two elements: a back cast which is made first, and a forward cast. You cannot make a good forward cast without making a back cast. At this stage you might think that casting with your back to the wind will help you cast further but, until you know how to make use of wind, it can be more of a hindrance than a help. But there are ways to increase casting distance which we will come to shortly. For the beginner, accuracy is far more important than length of cast.

When you make an overhead cast, the line first is thrown, or projected, backwards, then the rod is stopped so that the line can unroll behind the caster, and it is then thrown forwards and the rod stopped again so that the line can unroll out over the water. This brisk, crisp backwards and forwards motion generates energy in the fly line which in turn bends – or loads – the fly rod. It is the energy generated that propels the fly in the direction we determine. Some leading casters describe the casting motion as 'speed-up and stop'. Start moving your rod backwards, by raising your forearm and bending your elbow, slowly, then speed up and *stop* your rod by gripping the handle a little tighter and raising your elbow very slightly. Yes, stop. It can help to imagine that you

The line has unrolled and is about to drop onto the water

Good loops are essential to making a good cast

have a ball of putty or something similar stuck to your rod tip that you are trying to flick backwards or forwards. As you project, or throw, your line backwards and forwards, it forms a loop as it unrolls before changing direction. This is the casting loop. Loops can be big and wide, or small and tight. In general small, tight loops are what we are looking for as they produce more accurate (and longer) casts.

When your rod is loaded properly you should feel it bending right into your hand. You need to remember this feeling and aim to replicate it with each and every cast you make. You cannot make a cast – and load your rod – with slack line outside the tip ring. You must make the end of the line move across the water as this is the only way to eliminate slack in the line beyond the rod tip. If there is any, you waste the part of the casting stroke that is used to get the line moving and until you do that you will not have the full weight of line for the rod to load against. It is worth remembering that the back cast loads the rod, which then unloads when you stop the rod at the end of the back cast. You then have to load the rod again on the forward cast.

Casting is all about feeling, timing, having light hands, making the rod do the work and – *not trying too hard*. The last point cannot be stressed too many times.

Starting to cast

As well as wearing glasses to protect your eyes, never forget to check behind you to see if you might hit someone with your back cast. This can happen if you are fishing a piece of water where there are people walking about. You might need to wait before casting until a person has got clear of your back cast. Just as important, if you intend to walk behind a fellow angler, let him or her know that you are there so that he or she can keep back casts out of your way.

Once you have set up your rod and reel and threaded the line though the rod guides, hold your rod near the top with one hand while you pull some line off the reel and through the guides. You can let that line drop onto the ground or

riverbank. Now you need to take hold of the rod with the hand you are going to use to cast. That hand is known as your rod hand, and the other hand is your line hand. Hold the rod handle comfortably and firmly but not over-tightly. You are in charge of the rod and not the other way round. Some people hold their rod as though they are frightened of it. Don't be. The best way to hold your rod is as you would pick up a screwdriver or hammer.

The easiest way to hold a fly rod is as you would hold a hammer or screwdriver

It is easier to keep your wrist straight if you have your thumb on top of the rod handle

You can have your thumb on top of the rod handle – which has the benefit of making it slightly more difficult to bend your wrist – or to the side.

Some anglers may find it more comfortable to hold their rod with the thumb of their rod hand to the side, rather than on top

If you have the 'V' between your index finger and thumb aligned with the rod this will help you to keep your rod in line with your wrist and forearm. Your rod handle wants to be under your wrist. You must hold it firmly as you do not want it slipping or moving around in your hand, but do not hold it so tightly that it becomes uncomfortable. If you don't hold a screwdriver firmly you cannot drive a screw: your hand will turn but the screw won't. But beware of holding a rod too tightly as you will then overpower a cast, usually with disastrous results.

In the same way that you hold your rod as you would a hammer, the casting action is very similar to the action that you would use to knock a nail into a piece of wood. To do this successfully you need to hit the head of the nail with each blow of the hammer. Therefore you need to raise and lower the hammer head in exactly the same plane for each blow. You do this by keeping your upper arm by your side as you raise and lower your forearm and hand. When making a series of back and forward casts your rod hand needs to transcribe the same arc, without your upper arm flapping about, your wrist bending, or thrusting your hand forwards as you make your final presentation forward cast. As you use your forearm to lift your rod upwards and backwards, so throwing the line behind you, when your arm is at about forty-five degrees above horizontal, start to squeeze the rod handle, which will help you to accelerate the motion, and then raise your elbow and upper

The correct position for your rod hand at the end of a back cast. Rather similar to picking up a telephone to answer it

arm very slightly to bring everything to a smart halt. The combined actions of squeezing the rod handle at the same time as raising, or lifting, your elbow help speed-up your arm movement and bring the back cast to a precise and complete stop. Your rod hand should finish just by your eyebrow so that you can just see your thumb out of the corner of your eye.

After a brief pause while the line rolls out behind you, you can then punch the rod forward to make a forward, or presentation, cast. Again, start slowly and speed-up and stop. It is very important to ensure that your rod stays in the same vertical plane on both the back and forward casts.

You can stand with your feet placed firmly on the ground a comfortable distance apart square-on to where you are going to cast, which is called a closed stance, or your left foot forward (if you are casting with your right hand) which is known as an open stance.

The beginner will do well to start with a closed stance as it is better for making accurate casts, and these are what we want at this early stage. It will help the accuracy of your casts if you concentrate on and look where you want your fly to land: this is an important point to remember.

The roll cast

The second of the two basic casts is the roll cast. It is not only the easiest way for beginners to get a fly onto the water but it is also a very useful, practical fishing cast. You can use it to extend enough line to make an overhead cast or to get your line into position to make other casts. You can even use it to set the hook if a fish takes your fly very close to you. Because it is executed without a back cast, it can be used when there is no room to make a back cast and on days when there is a very strong wind behind you. This cast is easier to learn and practise on water as opposed to dry land as the surface tension on the fly line provides resistance, which is necessary to load your rod.

Start by feeding line out through the rod tip onto the water by waggling your rod from side to side, or use your hand to pull line off the reel. Hold the line against the rod handle with the index finger of your rod hand once you have got some line out. The tip of your rod should be pointing along the line and close to the ground, or water. Now raise your rod tip in a slow, continuous

Making a good roll cast is all about forming a good D-shaped loop with your fly line

Casting with a closed stance will help the beginner to cast more accurately

sweeping movement to the side and behind you, finishing with your hand up by your ear, with your thumb vertical. Your rod should be angled behind you by about forty-five degrees from the vertical. The fly line should be lying to the side of you and hanging from the rod tip in a 'D' loop.

You can stop with your rod and line in this position to check that you have formed a 'D' loop and that this loop is to your side. There must also be some line in front of you on the water, which must be stationary. If the line is still moving over the water, there will not be enough resistance to load the rod. You must make sure that you stop the line moving.

To complete the cast, punch your rod straight forward from your shoulder, using an action somewhat akin to hammering a nail into a piece of wood. Stop the rod at an angle of about forty degrees to the water so that the line can travel in the direction you want it to go. The loop will unroll and the line straighten out and then fall to the water. You complete the cast by following the line down with your rod tip.

You must aim your cast, whether a roll or over-head cast, above the water so that your fly drifts down and lands gently on the water. Aim your cast about 3 ft (90 cm) above the surface. If you aim too low, or straight at the water, your line and leader will slap down on the surface and create a disturbance that will frighten any fish nearby. The only time that you will aim your cast low is when you are casting into a strong headwind.

The overhead cast

The overhead cast with the line and rod moving rhythmically backwards and forwards is the classic cast that everyone associates with fly fishing. As well as being an iconic cast it is the cast that you will use most.

Start with the optimum 30 ft (9.1 m) of line on the grass or water and then trap the line against the rod handle with the index finger of your rod hand.

Just as you used only your rod hand to make a roll cast, it is easier to learn to make an overhead cast using one hand only. You can use a similar stance as for roll casting because you want to be able to make accurate casts. Your rod tip must be down by the water, or grass, and the line straight out in front of you. You now need to get the line moving so that it breaks the surface tension of the water and you are not trying to cast slack line, and then control its movement. You do this by using your forearm to raise the rod tip, slowly at

When starting to make a back cast hold the line firmly against the rod handle and don't let it slip

first and then speeding up – in a continuous movement – until your rod hand is about in line with your shoulder and level with your ear. Now STOP. *Squeeze* your rod to a stop – don't jerk it or bang it to a stop. And try not to bend your wrist when raising your rod: use your elbow so that you are casting – raising your rod – with your forearm rather than your wrist and hand. Remember what you read earlier about flicking a piece of putty off the tip of your rod as you raise your rod and throw the line upwards and behind you. Raising your upper arm slightly at the end of the back cast will help to ensure that the tip of your rod follows a straight line as you move it backwards and forwards. The path of travel should be similar to that of a paintbrush when painting a ceiling. To get the job done you want to keep the brush in contact with the ceiling for as long as possible, in a long, flat plane. A similar action with a fly rod will produce a tight loop. Tight loops are the most efficient and aerodynamic. And *squeezing* your rod to a stop helps produce tight loops. If you manipulate the brush in a convex curve, it will touch the ceiling only in the middle of the arc. If the rod tip follows a convex path the line will collide with the rod when you make a forward cast. When it follows a concave path, the result will be a tailing loop and a knot in your leader.

Just as you need to stop the movement of your casting arm at the end of the back cast, you need to make a definite pause before you start the forward, or presentation, cast. This pause is as crucial to making a good cast as stopping your rod. The pause is to allow the line to travel and unroll fully behind you. If you try to make your forward cast before the line is fully extended, you will be using your rod more like a whip than a fly rod and there will be a crack at the end of your line. (If this happens when you have a fly on the end of your line, you will lose it.) The energy generated by the line travelling backwards will eliminate the energy you are trying to generate on your forward cast and your line will end up in a tangle in front of you. How long to pause? The answer depends on a number of different factors, but the best thing to do is to turn your head and watch the line as it unrolls behind you. Turn your head again so that you are looking forwards

when you make your forward cast. As with the roll cast, aim the presentation cast above the water with your rod tip pointing slightly upwards from the horizontal. As the line starts to fall, follow it down with your rod tip.

Casting direction and wind

One of the fundamental principles of fly casting is that the line will always go in the direction the rod tip is pointing. This means that you point the rod at the end of the cast in the direction you want the line to go. But there is one time when this rule would seem not to hold true and that is casting when you have got a strong crosswind. To make a cast right up the middle of the river, you will have to compensate for the crosswind by aiming your cast either to the left, or the right, depending on which way the wind is blowing. Two things can go wrong: sometimes there will be a lull in the wind as you make your presentation cast, which means that you may have over-compensated for the wind, and second, if you are standing on the bank, as your line falls below the bank there will be no wind to blow it sideways. To deal with this problem you have to allow for the wind when making false casts (see below) but reduce that allowance as you make your presentation cast.

At the end of a back cast the rod handle should be no further from your wrist than the thickness of two fingers

False casts

Fly fishermen make what are known as false casts. A false cast is a cast, or series of backward and forward casts, when the line is kept in the air during both back cast and forward cast, not being allowed to land on the water in front of you during the latter. False casts with a short line can be made quicker than with a longer line. False casts can be made to dry a fly, work out more fly line, and to keep your fly in the air if you are trying to time your cast to a fish's feeding rhythm. Making false cast after false cast does not help you cast further. In fact the opposite will happen very often because, instead of generating and putting more energy into your rod and line, you run out of energy and your line will end up in an untidy pile close to your feet. Also, too much false casting is very likely to frighten fish as your line flies backwards and forwards over the water. Never, ever try to take part in the World False Casting Championship (it doesn't exist), which is won by the competitor making the most false casts. Should you really need to make a number of false casts, try to make them over the bank or at least not directly over a fish that you have seen or to which you are casting.

False casts are made in just the same way as a cast that will present your fly to a fish. You must

When casting use your line hand to hold and control the line. It is important to know how to use your line hand properly when casting, and to understand the role that it plays

make a back cast with the speed-up and stop motion of your casting arm. Then stop, pause to allow the line to unroll and then make a forward cast again starting slowly, speeding up and stopping your rod.

And remember the ideal number of false casts is ONE per cast. Never make more false casts than absolutely essential.

Using your line hand

You started casting by ignoring your line hand and holding the line trapped against the rod handle when executing both a roll cast and an overhead cast. Now it is time to bring your line hand into play.

The line hand plays a very important role in casting as well as being used to retrieve your line: much more than many people realize. When casting you need to hold the line firmly so that the rod can work against its weight. Letting the line slip through your fingers will not load your rod properly and if you don't load your rod you will not be able to make a good cast. Your line hand anchors the line and also controls it if you are increasing line length while false casting. Your rod hand holds the rod only. When you release line on the forward cast, do not simply let go of or drop the line thereby losing control of it. If you do, you will have to look down to take hold of it again. Form a ring with either your first finger and thumb, or your first and second fingers, and let the line flow through that ring. You can now keep the line under control and if you realize that your cast is going wrong, you can grip the line and make another back cast and a better or correct forward cast. If you lose control of the line and look down to find it, you will have to take your eyes off the fish. Should the fish rise and take your fly as it touches the water, you will not be able to set the hook straight away. And it will also be difficult to start retrieving your line straight away.

As you lift the line off the water and make a back cast, you should aim to keep a constant distance between your hands, with your line hand at a comfortable height. *What you do* with your line hand is more important than having it in a precise or specific position.

When you are fishing, as you complete the presentation cast, bring your line hand – and the line – up to the rod handle so that you can hook the line behind the index finger of your rod hand and hold the line against the rod handle. As you retrieve line with your other hand, you need to release and trap the line, in turn, against the rod handle.

Making changes to casting loops

There are three casting loops: open non-loops, tight loops and tailing loops. The path of the rod tip as it travels backwards and then forwards, dictates what type of loop you create. To make an open loop the tip of your rod wants to follow a convex path so that at the end of both back cast and forward it will be low, which will produce a wide loop. Open loops are not always bad. The one time when an open loop can be a benefit is on the forward cast with a strong tail-wind. The wind will catch the line and blow it forward.

A tight loop looks like a condensed 'U' on its side, so that the top and bottom parts of the line are close together and roughly parallel. They are formed by stopping the travel of the rod when it is still high. The tip of your rod should take a straight path between the stop at the end of the back cast and the stop at the end of the forward cast. Conversely, stopping the rod lower on the back cast, or forward cast, will result in a wider loop. This can also be achieved by making the rod tip take a convex path, rather than a straight one, as mentioned.

Tailing loops result from bad casting, so they are not loops that we strive to make, unless an instructor, for example, wants to demonstrate how one comes about to a pupil. A tailing loop is a loop where the top part of the loop falls below the bottom part and on the forward cast the fly, leader or line catches the bottom of the loop, often resulting in a knot and a bad cast. They result from overpowering the forward cast and when the rod tip follows a concave path. Power (at this stage of the learning process) and excessive energy are not needed, but feeling, rhythm and smooth movements are. Remember, it's the rod that does the work, not the caster.

Altering the angle of the casting arc

Although your casting arc should be parallel to the water, it is quite easy to alter the angle. For example, you might want to make a higher back cast so that your line is clear of an obstacle behind you. You can achieve this by tilting the casting arc forwards: stop your back cast a bit sooner and extend your forward cast down a little more. And to make a higher forward cast, simply tilt the casting arc backwards.

When you start your first cast with the line on the ground or on the water, your rod hand will move through a much longer or wider arc than on subsequent false casts. The length of casting arc is just one of many variables in fly fishing. Short arc, or stroke, for short casts, and a longer stroke for longer casts.

Practice

It is very easy to practise casting at home. If you have not got a garden that is big enough to practice in, then don't be embarrassed about using your local park or a playing field. You'll soon get used to silly comments and you may even meet a fellow fly fisher. Tie a piece of wool to the end of your leader so that you can see it, and to stop it

Once you have grasped the basics of casting it will become possible to add versatility to your casting by altering the angle of the arc you make when casting. Here the angler is making a high back cast

65

When practising casting always aim your casts at a target as this will help you to develop good accuracy

CASTING MISTAKES

One of the most common mistakes made – and one of the easiest to make – is trying too hard. Trying and succeeding in using too much power when casting will result in a tailing loop and casting knots in your leader or tippet, as we have just seen. You can also end-up with your fly caught around the end of your line. Avoiding trying too hard is a point that cannot be repeated too often. You need to make the rod and line do the work, and keep in control. Try not to thrust your rod arm forwards when you make the final presentation cast as it doesn't add any extra distance to your cast. After a while you will find that good casting develops a feeling, rhythm and sound and if one of these changes, you will realize that something is not quite right. If the sound of a cast changes to a fluttering sound, it may be because you have flicked a leaf off a tree, hooked a blade of grass on your back cast – or even a dragonfly!

Other circumstances; other types of cast

Now it is time to look at some other useful, practical fishing casts that will help you to overcome problems which affect your ability to cast, and those caused by where a fish might be lying in a river.

cracking. You want to practise in all weathers, not just calm days. On windy days, practise casting into the wind, with the wind and with the wind blowing from either side. Cast with an obstacle behind you and cast under a tree or bush if available. For accuracy, try casting at a plate or similar. Move your target about so the distance that you have to cast varies, and change the angle of your casts as well.

A very useful cast made by tilting your rod across your body so that the rod tip and line pass over your other shoulder.

OFF-THE-SHOULDER CAST

The off-the-shoulder cast is very useful when fishing on the 'wrong' bank (that is when your line hand, rather than your rod hand, is next to the river), or when there is an obstruction or a strong crosswind (on both rivers and stillwaters) so that the line, as you cast, is being blown onto you rather than to the side and away from you.

You make this cast just the same as a normal overhead cast but you tilt your rod across the front of your body so that the rod tip and line pass over your other shoulder. If you angle your forearm across your body, you will end the back cast element with your rod and hand by your opposite ear.

It can also help if you stand with your right foot (for right-hand casters) forward, rather than your left foot. You can make a slightly less extreme cast by casting over your head so that your hand is in front of your face on the back cast.

SIDE-ARM CAST

The side-arm cast can be helpful when casting to fish in challenging lies, particularly underneath overhanging branches or bushes, or under a bridge. It is exactly the same cast as an over-

head cast but made at ninety degrees and parallel to the water. It is not a cast you will use that frequently but when you do need to use it, you will be pleased that you know how to. Its main problem is keeping the back cast clear of bankside vegetation, but this is less of a problem if you are wading in a river. It is also a useful cast on very windy days, again when wading, as you can keep your back and forward casts close to the water where there is less wind to influence things. It is also a good cast to make when you want to keep your rod low so that it is less likely to spook fish, or to keep false casts out of sight of fish.

Whereas the off-the-shoulder cast is made with your rod angled across your body at around forty-five degrees, with the side-arm cast your rod and casting arm are at ninety degrees to your body. To do this more easily it will help if you stand with your back foot a little further back.

DEALING WITH STRONG WINDS

Casting on very windy days is always a big challenge but extra line speed, tight loops and keeping your cast low can all help, as can the reverse cast. One of the most important points is to try to cast in the lulls which occur even with

Although kneeling down gives you more clearance to make a cast under the canopy of trees, it does mean that your rod and line are that much closer to the water as you make a side cast. Overcoming one problem creates another

Left At the end of the back cast of an off-the-shoulder cast your rod hand will be by your opposite ear

the strongest of winds. And the reverse is true: try not to cast in a strong gust. Strong winds can hamper your back cast just as much as your forward cast. You make a reverse cast by turning round so that you face in the opposite direction to where you want your cast to go. If you do this when the wind is blowing on your back, you will make your forward cast into the wind and your presentation cast behind you but *with* the wind. As mentioned earlier, you can eliminate the back cast by using a roll cast.

Casting into a headwind is most anglers' nightmare. But as long as the line is unrolling out in front of you, it is moving forwards and it will only be stopped, or blown back, when it has straightened fully. A tight loop is more aero-dynamic than an open loop and will, therefore, travel faster and more easily into the wind. As well as trying to cast with tighter loops, it helps to aim your cast lower. This is because any waves or ripples on the water create friction which slows the wind slightly so that you can aim a lower cast under the worst of the wind.

The key to casting with strong winds is angling your casting arc. With a tail wind you need to end your back cast with your hand

Shooting line – releasing slack line hanging down between your line hand and the reel – helps you to make much longer casts

Jérôme Philipon

behind your ear, rather than by it. This gives you a longer back cast stroke and, if the wind slows the rearward travel of your line, because you will have to make a longer forward cast, you will still be able to load your rod. It will also help if you end your forward cast with the rod lower and closer to the water than normal. This has the effect of driving the line downwards as well as forwards.

MAKING LONGER CASTS

When casting, a process called shooting line helps you make a longer cast. This means that you can make false casts – to dry your fly for example – without your line passing over the fish to which you want to cast and possibly frightening it – but still reach the target area when you make your presentation cast. Shooting line involves releasing slack line hanging down between your line hand and the reel just as you stop the rod on the forward casting stroke and the line extends in front of you.

As you gain experience you will be able to shoot a significant amount of line. To shoot line you do not need to move your line hand: simply release the line and let it run through the circle formed by your thumb and first finger. Don't drop the line and let it shoot without any control: if you do, you risk the line getting in a tangle. Practice will soon help you to release the line at the right moment. If, as you shoot line, you judge that your fly is going to land too far from the fish or perhaps on the riverbank, you can stop the line by grip-ping it between your thumb and fingers.

Although shooting line is usually associated with the final forward, or presentation, cast, you can shoot line on the back cast as well. You do this in the same way by releasing some line when you stop the rod and then holding the line tight as you make a forward cast.

One of the most important things you can do with your line hand is using it to make either a single or double haul. Making a haul – pulling the line with your line hand – increases line speed, which not only helps you make longer casts, but can also help make a medium-length cast if you can only make a short casting stroke. Getting your line moving faster produces quicker casts which will be less affected by the wind and will be more accurate. Hauls also help line control, which is such an important part of being able to cast proficiently. Hauls do not have to be so long that you have to extend your arm fully to the side. An efficient haul can be made by pulling the line as little 6–8 in (15–20 cm), as long as the timing is right and it is made quickly. A single haul is one where you pull on the line on the back cast only; a double haul is where you pull on the line on both the back cast and forward cast.

To make a single haul or double haul you must start with your rod hand and line hand moving together. You make the haul once you have started moving your rod, and not before. As you lift the fly line off the water and start to make your back cast, your line hand follows your rod hand up and back. What happens next – when you make the first haul – can best be described in one word coined by one of America's foremost fly casting experts: 'downup'. Your hand pulls down on the line (and away from your rod hand) and then returns without a pause to where it started the pull, or haul, so your hands are back together again and the line is kept under tension all the time. And you repeat the process in exactly the same way as you make the forward cast: hands moving forward together, followed by another 'downup' movement of your line hand that finishes with your hands together. Hauls of whatever length should be make positively and briskly. The speed of the haul should mirror the acceleration of the rod on both casts.

To get your timing right, you must remember that your hands must be back together at the end of each casting stroke. This means that you can start a short haul of 6–8 in (15–20 cm) later in the casting stroke compared to a longer haul. When you want to shoot line for the final presentation cast, you make the haul – the 'down' part of 'downup' – but instead of returning your line hand to be with your rod hand, you release the line and let it shoot out through the rod rings.

A good way to teach yourself how to double haul is to start on a lawn or grass field and practise making back casts first and then forward casts, both with a haul. Once you have got the feeling you can then start to join the two casts together.

You must use an open stance when making a double haul cast. A closed stance will restrict arm and body movement

Making good double haul casts requires good timing and making the hauls at the right stage of the back cast and forward cast

CHAPTER FIVE

Fish food: what fish feast on

Trout have a very catholic taste when it comes to feeding, and an intake of food that is able to cope with times of plenty, such as hatches of mayflies, and famine during the winter when there can often seem to be very little life in a river or stream.

As well as having a catholic taste, trout are predatory, opportunistic feeders and so spend much of their time looking out for tasty morsels. For any fish to grow and put on weight, it must consume more energy in the form of food than it expends finding and eating that food. It also needs somewhere to live that does not drain it of energy. Fish eat most of their food below the surface in the form of nymphs, caddis larvae and pupae, freshwater shrimps, snails, pea mussels, small baitfish

and even crayfish. An interesting example of this is in Argentina where there is a type of crayfish, the Patagonian false crab, known as pancoras, which is an important source of food for big brown trout. Apparently you can tell when a fish has been feeding on them as its stomach feels as though it is full of stones. The fact that fish spend most of their time feeding below the surface is the reason why fishing below the surface is so important and can be so effective (see Chapter 8). But, to concentrate on flies: fish start to feed on the surface on flies that have hatched from a nymph or caddis larva when a hatch of flies gets underway.

Hatches of fly can range from very sparse, with only a few flies hatching, often for only a few minutes, through a more significant hatch lasting

Jérôme Philipon

A newly-hatched mayfly drying its wings on streamside vegetation

longer (perhaps for up to half an hour), to inter-mittent or spasmodic hatches over an extended period, up to a major hatch lasting for a number of hours. A further problem is that a hatch can be limited to quite a short stretch of water and if you are not there at the right time, you may think that no flies have hatched. The length and intensity of hatches of up-winged flies and caddis varies from river to river, and according to time of day, the weather and the season.

Another group of insects that provide food for fish are terrestrial flies including hawthorns in the spring, crane flies (or daddy-long-legs), grasshoppers and various small beetles. These are land insects that are either blown onto the water or fall from bankside vegetation. They can be a very significant and important source of food for fish at certain times of the year.

All fly fishers need to have a basic under-standing of what fish might be feeding on and when – and where – as this will help in the selec-tion of a suitable artificial fly to fish.

Some forms of fly food are of more relevance and importance to the fly fisher than others. Sometimes you may need to fish a very specific

size and pattern of fly – usually referred to as 'matching the hatch' – while at other times a generic pattern – something that imitates every-thing in general but nothing in particular – will prove to be very effective.

It is helpful and very interesting to see the differences in colours of nymphs and caddis larvae and the great variation in sizes. The way to do this is by what is called kick sampling, which involves kicking the riverbed, or clumps of weed, and catching the bugs that are disturbed in a net.

Anglers can use kick sampling before a day's fishing or on a regular basis, perhaps once a month

Although there are many thousands of different patterns of artificial flies, most anglers use very few patterns on a regular basis

Weeds harbour invertebrates that fish feed on and so are essential to the health and well-being of trout streams

Special nets, made with a metal hoop and a very fine net, are used by fly-life researchers, but a simple net can be made with a piece of net curtain attached to two lengths of broom handle or dowelling. In use the net is held close to the riverbed while you stand upstream and disturb the bed with your feet. What is caught by or in the net can be emptied into a shallow tray for examination. This is something that the keen angler can do at the start of the day so that he or she can see what nymphs, etc., are in a river and how active they are. The Riverfly Partnership, an ongoing project based on this practice, was launched in England in March 2007, to help and encourage anglers to carry out health checks on their rivers using monitoring techniques to detect any severe changes in water quality. Changes could be highlighted by a reduction in numbers or absence of species of the main groups of river flies that anglers imitate when fly fishing. Working with a group of like-minded anglers is not only a very good way of keeping a check on water quality but it is also one of the very best ways to learn and discover more about aquatic flies.

Up-winged flies

Up-winged flies (flies with upright wings) are some of the most obvious flies to be seen on rivers and lakes and are, in many ways, of most interest and importance to fly fishermen. Adult

flies mate and then the females lay their eggs either underwater or on the surface, from where they will sink to the riverbed. These eggs will hatch into nymphs.

The nymphs then make their way to the surface, where they hatch into up-winged flies known as duns, which are the flies that can be seen on the surface of a river or lake. These newly hatched, air-breathing flies – sub-imagoes – have to dry their wings before they can fly off. Sometimes they get stuck, and in any case while this

Flies that get stuck in the surface film and do not manage to take off make an easy meal for a hungry fish

drying is happening they are very vulnerable to becoming a tasty morsel for a hungry fish.

If they survive this process, these duns leave the water to mutate into fully mature adults, known as imagoes or spinners, which are capable of reproduction.

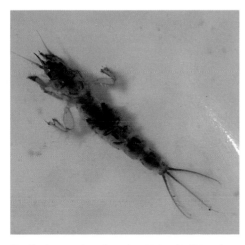

Trout feed on nymphs as they swim about and as they make their way to the surface where they will hatch into adult flies

A mayfly spinner takes a rest on the side of a car some way from the river

73

After laying their eggs, the spent females can often be seen lying on the surface with their wings stretched out either side of their body, where they will be joined by the adult males.

Nymphs develop underwater for periods ranging from as little as three months to up to two years for the mayfly, during which time they shed their exoskeletons and grow new bigger ones. Nymphs are vulnerable to being eaten by fish at any stage of their life and anywhere from the riverbed to the surface where they hatch. Hatching nymphs are at their most vulnerable as they struggle out of their nymphal case, as they have no means of making an escape.

Nymphs in the process of hatching into adult flies are knowns as emergers by anglers

Anglers classify nymphs into four main categories: agile darters or swimmers, laboured swimmers, stone clingers and bottom burrowers. All these names are descriptive of the way they move or where they like to live. Typical agile darters are the nymphs of baetids, which move and swim with surprising speed, enough to swim against the current. Laboured swimmers, which are neither great swimmers nor particularly good clingers, include many different families, such as nymphs of the Leptophlebiidae and Tricorythodes. Stone clingers show many variations, including adaptations to live in slower waters, but are generally found in fast-flowing rivers where their flatter form with strong legs and claws helps them cling on to the river bed. The best-known bottom burrower is without doubt the nymph of the mayfly (*Ephemera danica* or *E. vulgata*) which is known as the Greendrake (*E. guttulata*) in the USA.

Caddis and their life cycle

There are many different types of caddis – hundreds in fact. Only relatively few of them are of interest to anglers, but that does not reduce their importance. In contrast to the up-wings, which live for only hours or a day or two at most, in their adult form caddis can live for a week or more as they can drink and so do not suffer from dehydration. The fact that you can see adult caddis fly around should not always be taken as a sign that it is time to tie on a caddis imitation, as it is quite likely that they are doing nothing more than enjoying a good fly around. The caddis that are of interest to the trout – and anglers – are

The tent-shaped wings of a caddis, or sedge, make them very easy to distinguish from up-wing flies

pupae drifting with the current just below the surface prior to emerging as fully formed adults, and egg-laying females diving underwater to lay their eggs.

Adult caddis have tent-shaped wings lying over their backs, no tails, and some have very long, prominent antennae. Their wings are soft and hairy. This makes them very easy to recognize. Some skitter over the surface, particularly while laying eggs, while most can be seen buzzing about in a blur of wings, just above the water.

Caddis, unlike mayflies, go through what is known as a complete metamorphosis, starting from the egg stage, going through larval and then pupal stages before emerging as the complete air-breathing adult. They are very

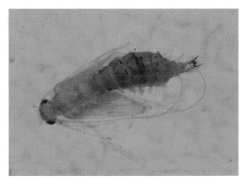

The pupal stage is the last that a caddis goes through before turning into an air-breathing adult

interesting little creatures: some are free-swimming and are known as case-less; others build often complex cases from tiny bits of gravel, grains of sand, shells and the like and are known as cased caddis. Others create cases that look

Case-less caddis can be found in a range of colours and sizes

Cased caddis are the most unusual and extraordinary of the many different caddis. As they grow they need to make a bigger case

like tiny bits of twig and some make cases, or nets, out of self-produced silk. Some cases are attached to tiny bits of vegetation while others will be glued to stones on the riverbed. The inhabitants of these splendid cases outgrow them on a regular basis and when they leave them to start building a bigger case, they are vulnerable to hungry trout. But other species will refurbish their case to cope with growth! Cased caddis larvae are predatory and will eat quite large mayfly nymphs.

Many female caddis dive underwater to lay their eggs on the stream bottom, while others crawl down pieces of weed or vegetation to do this. Caddis that lay their eggs on the surface can do this either by dipping their abdomens into the water or by landing on the water and fluttering around. Yet again there are caddis that float along quite happily, laying eggs as they go.

Caddis can demonstrate very interesting behaviour known as behavioural drift. This happens when, at the same time, large numbers of pupae release their grip on the bottom of a river or stream and get washed along by the current. This can happen on a daily basis, often around dusk or before dawn, and while the angler may not be able to see this happening, the immature caddis are easy prey for hungry fish.

A stone covered in dozens of cased caddis. In shallow water it is easy to pick up stones like this so that you can examine them closely

75

Stoneflies

Stoneflies are another order of insects of interest to anglers. They are generally found in faster-flowing rivers. When they are present in a river or stream they can be of real significance to anglers. Just to be different from other species, stoneflies develop through three stages only, namely egg, nymph and adult. Stonefly nymphs are chunky things and, importantly, have only two shortish tails (up-wing nymphs have three longish tails). If stonefly nymphs were mayflies or up-wings, they would all be classified as clingers. They are equipped with double claws on their legs, which help them grip and clamber over rocks, and many of them have flattened bodies to make clinging even easier. They are poor swimmers so if they lose their hold on the riverbed, either accidentally or during behavioural drift, they become prime targets for trout.

Stoneflies, with some exceptions, emerge by crawling out of the water onto sticks, stones, pieces of timber or other objects by the bank. Some species will emerge immediately on leaving the water, while others will crawl some way away. Many of them will go on to live quite long lives as they can eat and drink. They carry their wings over their backs – like caddis – but they lie flat instead of in an inverted 'V'.

Terrestrials

Terrestrials are land-based insects that only become of interest to fish when they fall or are blown onto the water. Everyone must know what a crane fly, or daddy-long-legs, looks like and therefore it is easy to identify a suitable artificial fly to fish if these insects are flying and falling onto the water – you need an artificial with long dangly legs. Another terrestrial fly that is easy to identify is the hawthorn, which hatches in the spring in the UK, when the field and roadside hedges are in blossom. Hawthorns are black, laboured fliers with legs that hang down. When there are plenty of hawthorns flying around on a windy day, sport can be very good as the poor things get blown onto the water and they can't take off. Once on the water their transparent wings can often be seen lying over the back of

their bodies. Beetles living on bankside vegetation can often fall onto the water in large numbers. They can be difficult to see as they can be quite small and are often floating *in* the surface film, rather than *on* it. Do keep an eye on bankside vegetation where you may see iridescent beetles, adult caddis and all sorts of other insects.

Fish lying close to the bank will feed on little beetles like these when they lose their grip and fall into the water

Stillwater insects

For stillwater anglers one of the most important forms of trout food are the many hundreds of species of chironomids that form the order of Diptera or true flies, like house flies and mosquitoes. They are one of the most common food forms in stillwaters at almost any time of the year. Hatches of Chironomidae can be so prolific that they fill the air. Chironomidae eggs develop into larvae, often known as bloodworms, which live in the silty depths of stillwaters, then into pupae which are termed buzzers by anglers, and finally the adult winged insect. The adults, which have two wings only, are of little or no interest as they leave the water so quickly once hatched.

Once they have hatched, the adults swarm and mate in flight and the females lay eggs on vegetation or on the bottom of the lake. Some eggs hatch into larvae that form mud tubes, while others, such as the bloodworm, are free swimming. The larvae, which are worm-like with segmented bodies, grow and develop into pupae which, when fully developed, make their way to the surface by wiggling. Some larvae swim with a writhing, thrashing action. A pupa will hang vertically while it rests before continuing its wiggly way to the surface. At the surface it will take some minutes to break through the surface film and hatch. The pupae are vulnerable to being eaten by trout at all stages from the bottom to the point of hatching. The pupae develop an eye spot, wing casing and white gills, near the head, which are their most prominent feature. Pupae

Adult damsel flies are very easy to recognize. Trout will often feed on them when they are flying close to the water's surface by leaping out of the water and grabbing them in mid-air

can be found in a wide range of colours including black, brown, reddy-brown and green.

Suspender buzzer patterns were developed to mimic the way chironomid pupae are often found suspended, or hanging, vertically in the water. This is a very important point to remember, as a fly fished horizontally does not look or act like a live pupa.

Damsel and dragonfly nymphs are also popular with trout as they can be found in lakes all year round. Damsel nymphs are aggressive below the water and, once hatched into adults, they feed on other flies and will even attack and consume flies as big as mayflies.

Other forms of food include shrimps, snails,

Corixae or water boatmen and terrestrials at certain times of the year and when the wind is blowing in the right direction. Stillwaters also have hatches of caddis and up-wings, including mayfly, which will provide good sport when they are hatching. Even if no adult flies can be seen on the surface, the nymphs could well be active.

Fish fry

In addition to eating insects, trout are also fry feeders at certain times of the season when fry are in abundance. Most stillwaters of any reasonable size will contain small fish species and the young of various coarse fish. Although fry-feeding is of more relevance to the stillwater angler than the river angler, trout will eat minnows and fry in rivers. On the first day of a recent season the treasurer of my fishing club caught a lovely big trout that had four minnows in its mouth. Was that five fish for the price of one? Or five fish on one fly? Trout feeding on fry in stillwaters may be seen chasing shoals of them very close to the surface and fry will even jump out of the water as they attempt to escape being eaten. Some fry may be killed or stunned by this behaviour and as they float on the surface they will be an easy meal for a fish.

A damsel makes a meal of a mayfly and so brings its brief life to a premature end. Damsels are aggressive carnivores and like nothing better than making a meal of a mayfly. You will often see them swoop on newly hatched mayflies and start to devour them

CHAPTER SIX

Savour the moment: your first days on the river

We are at last heading off for our first day on the river: the start of a great adventure and a moment to savour.

Now that you are ready to have your first day on the water, when is the best time to go fishing? The quick and easy answer is whenever you can. If you don't go fishing, you won't catch fish. But some times of the day are better than others, depending to some extent on the time of the year. Apart from perhaps the very hottest days of the season, I would always try to fish between mid-morning and mid-afternoon. Some days the afternoon will prove more productive than the morning and vice versa. Do resist the temptation to leave the river and go to the pub for lunch – you may miss the best fishing of the day. In high summer it can be better to fish either in the late afternoon and evening or, if you are a morning person, to get up with the sun and enjoy peace and tranquillity as the sun rises and burns off any early morning mist.

After a while you may meet anglers who make excuses or come up with too many reasons for not going fishing simply to disguise their likely failure to catch a fish. Try to ignore them. They will say that it is far too sunny – yes, fishing on sunny days can be very challenging (more on this shortly) – or that it is too cold, too hot or too windy. Strong winds can certainly make casting difficult but they can have their compensations. Towards the end of one April a spell of strong northerly and north-easterly winds, blowing down the valley of a river I know very well, produced the most fantastic falls of hawthorns. They were hatching in the rough grassland, hedgerows and around the edges of woodland and then being blown across the meadows and falling onto the water, where the hungry trout were waiting for them eagerly. They are not strong fliers and once on the water they are trapped and unable to take off. Fish were rising all the time that the hawthorns were arriving, and were being caught on well-presented imitations. Without these strong winds and a good hatch of hawthorns, we would never have had these days of spectacular fishing so early in the season. So anyone who was put off going fishing because of the winds missed some really good and exciting days.

When you arrive at the river for the first time you will, of course, want to have a look at it as quickly as possible. Do this by all means, but do not simply rush straight to the bank or onto a bridge and lean over to look into the water.

What could be more inviting? A clear chalk stream under a cloudless blue sky. On a day like this when line and rod flash may frighten fish, try to take advantage of any clouds that hide the sun

Jérôme Philipon

The fish that made this small and rather insignificant rise was a fine wild brown trout that was feeding on hatching iron blue duns

Instead, approach the river slowly and carefully so that you do not frighten any fish in your immediate vicinity. A quiet, gentle approach will give you a much better chance of spotting a fish or two and seeing what is happening – whether any fish are rising or flies hatching – compared to an over-hasty approach. Be stealthy in your movements and approach and stay alert at all times for anything that happens in the river and on the surface. Just because you see what seems to be a tiny rise, don't assume that it is a small fish. Sometimes the biggest fish will leave the smallest rise-form as it sips-in a fly very delicately and leaves very little disturbance on the surface.

One of the keys to fishing successfully is to have confidence that you *will* catch a fish. Obviously, when you start you have only limited knowledge of what you are supposed to be doing and your sense of confidence may be non-existent – or very high – depending on your personality! And even experienced anglers can lack confidence quite often because of a lack of knowledge of how to approach and fish a river or stream. But it does help to fish with conviction, commitment and determination. Confidence comes with practice, with following tried and tested methods and using tackle and equipment

suitable for the water to be fished. For the beginner, choosing a fly to use is a major challenge. You can make your choice easier by starting with a small selection of proven fish-catchers. When you catch your first fish, you will then probably want to use the same fly again. It caught one fish so it will *definitely* catch another because you will fish it with supreme confidence. In due course you will find that there are times when a change in the size of fly is more important than a change of pattern.

Preparations at home and at the river

It is all too easy for the newcomer to fly fishing to leave home in a state of great excitement and arrive at the river to find that they have left their rod, reel or some other vital piece of equipment behind. So make yourself a checklist (a mental one is better than no list) of everything that you need to take with you and use it as you put your tackle and equipment into your car. Tackle, clothing, camera, food and drink. Get into the habit of loading everything into your car in the same order and place. This may sound tedious but it could save you a ruined day.

Do make sure that you have got everything in your car before setting off to the river or stillwater. This may stop you leaving some vital piece of tackle behind

When you have arrived at the river and parked your car in a safe place, you can change into your fishing clothing and then put your tackle together. Once you have done that and are ready to head for the water, always make sure that you have not left a rod tube or any other item of tackle in your car where it can be seen, particularly if you have parked in a lonely spot.

It is also worth considering whether it is a good idea to put any fishing tackle makers' or other angling stickers on your car. Both could attract the attention of a passing 'anti' or an

The new angler will find his or her first days on the river much more rewarding in the company of a knowledgeable friend

opportunist car thief. And do make sure you know where your car key is. One evening I arrived back at my car, put my hand in my pocket to get the key to unlock the car and there was no key. Something made me start to take off my waders and when I pulled them down, I found my key! When I had reached inside my waders to put the key in my trouser pocket, instead of putting it in my pocket, I missed and it went down the leg of my waders. I was very relieved not to have lost it.

Approaching the river

WHY WE FISH UPSTREAM

It is important to understand this point before surveying a stretch of water or starting to fish.

Fishing upstream means that you approach fish from behind so they have less chance of seeing you. Some clubs have a rule that prohibits fishing downstream

Jérôme Philipon

We fish upstream because trout spend their lives facing into the current, looking forwards (upstream) for items of food that are being brought down by the current, and, therefore, the angler approaching them from behind is very much less likely to be seen compared to one who is casting or fishing downstream in full view of a fish. Another important reason for fishing upstream is that when a fish takes your fly, as you raise your rod to set the hook you are more likely to pull the fly back into its mouth, whereas when fishing downstream the pull is upstream, directly away from the fish and out of its mouth. Fishing upstream means that on a river you will need to start at the bottom of the beat or piece of water that you intend to fish because you will be moving upstream all the time. Because you are fishing against the current, when your fly lands on or in the water, the current brings it back to you.

MOVEMENT ON THE BANK

When you arrive at the river you may decide that you are going to fish the water by where you are standing, or you might want to make your way slowly and carefully along the bank until you come to where you think is a better place to fish. Some people like to keep busy by casting regularly and, in so doing, covering plenty of water, while others will take a more contemplative approach and sit and watch the water, waiting for a fish to betray its presence in some way and fishing only what they consider, or hope, will be the best bits.

If you have parked at the bottom of the beat, then you can probably start fishing almost straight away, after a few minutes spent observing what is happening. But if you have parked halfway up or at the top of the beat, you will have to make your way to the bottom. Always try to keep well back from the water so that you don't frighten fish. Unfortunately, there are some rivers and beats where the only way to get to the bottom is to walk along the riverbank, next to the water. In such cases, all you can do is walk along as quickly and unobtrusively as possible. All being well, by the time that you are ready to make your first casts, some of the fish nearest to you will have recovered from the shock of your presence on the bank. If the river is fenced, it is best not to walk between the fence and the bank unless you have to. If you do you will scare virtually every fish in the river. So keep well back from the edge of the bank at all times when you are not actually fishing so that you can keep out of sight of the fish.

When you are walking about with your rod assembled, which is the best way to carry it? You will hold it at the point of balance, which is usually by the handle, but should the tip point forwards or backwards? One school of thought says that the rod tip should always be held pointing back-wards so that if you stumble and fall, the rod handle, not the tip, will hit the ground. But one disadvantage of carrying a rod behind you is that, when walking between bushes or under trees, the line can get caught by a twig or branch – which is a nuisance. If you walk with your rod tip in front of you, you must make sure that you keep it pointing upwards and not down at the ground. It can also be easier to thread the tip between bushes and branches. In practice a combination of both ways, depending on where you are, is likely to be the best.

Whenever you move along a riverbank, as well as keeping back from the edge, do so quietly and carefully. Some days on some rivers you may not see another angler, but if there is another angler fishing, keep well way when you pass by so that you do not get in the way and you do not frighten the fish for which he or she is fishing. If you have no choice but to pass close by, do give notice of your presence by a gentle cough or whistle, and be prepared to wait for a good moment before you pass. If you are moving back downstream, keep well away from the bank as there is nothing more annoying than fishing your way quietly upstream towards a favourite stretch and then seeing someone marching along by the water, frightening all the fish, without a care in the world or a thought for anyone else. Treat other anglers with the same respect and regard that you would wish them to show to you. Unfor-tunately, not everyone will return the compliment but at least you will know how to behave properly.

WHICH BANK?

There will be a number of factors to consider when deciding which bank to fish when there is a choice. Some beats will have access on one bank only, which may or may not be the 'right' bank for you (when your casting arm is next to the water). As explained earlier, given a choice of which bank to fish, most people will fish so that their casting arm is next to the river, as this is the easier way to cast and fish. However, there are other factors to consider. Wind direction can be significant, as can the position of the sun, which affects what you can see in the water and where your shadow falls if the sun is high in the sky. Sometimes, consideration of these two factors may mean that, in practice, it will be better to fish from the 'wrong', or less favoured, bank. Also, of

It's easy to forget that when the sun is behind you your shadow may fall right across the river

Although bankside trees and vegetation can be a nuisance, they add to the challenge of catching fish in small streams. They provide cover for fish as well as a source of food

course, your ability to cast easily and accurately is going to be affected by trees or bankside vegetation. When you are fishing where there are trees on the banks, don't forget to check every now and then that your back cast isn't going to catch a branch.

STARTING TO FISH

Once you have decided where to fish, try to think like a hunter and move slowly and deliberately

Before casting to a fish that you can see rising on the other side of the river, try to make sure that you are not going to frighten a fish closer to you

like a heron. Consider the best way to approach a piece of water rather than rushing up to the bank and starting to cast. As you get into position to make your first cast, take care not to wave your rod about over the water, particularly on sunny days when the glint or flash from it may spook a fish, or the shadow that it casts upsets a fish. If you have to turn round, turn away from the water rather than towards it, so keeping your rod over land and not water.

On an ideal day you will be able to start casting to a feeding fish, but you should always start by making your first casts close to your own bank – unless there is a really good reason to cast to the middle of the river or the far bank such as a rising fish – because there may well be fish close to your feet. If you cast straight across the river you will probably frighten fish that you have not seen. If there are fish to be seen under or close to the far bank, there is every reason to expect to find fish by your bank. If you are planning to wade a section of river always fish your way into the river by making a few casts around the area where you intend to get into the water. If you simply get in you may frighten fish close to the bank, which will rush off upstream frightening other fish as they go.

If you are fishing a wide river it can help to divide it into sections to make it more manageable. Then fish each section thoroughly, starting from by your bank and working your way across the river, section by section. For each section start by casting upstream as though towards twelve o'clock on a clock face and then through one o'clock to two o'clock and then three. Do this for each section in turn. If you see no fish or do not get an offer from one, take two or three steps along the bank so that you can start casting to a different piece of the river or stream. Should a fish rise to your fly or show interest in it, concentrate on that fish with accurate casts. If it is a sporting fish that takes your fly – wonderful. If it is uncooperative or you frighten it, move on to another one. When is the best time to move along the bank? There are a number of options. You can move just as you are about to make another cast, that is when you have fished it out, or when your fly has passed the fish you were aiming for. If you have just made a cast and a fish rises further upstream, you may want to move straight away so that you can get close to that fish. But if you do this, make sure that you have your line properly under control and are ready to set the hook if a fish rises to your fly.

WHEN THERE IS NO RESPONSE

There will be days when you can spend quite a lot of time casting to one (or sometimes more) fish without getting any response. It could be that it is not feeding or it may even be asleep. The problem is to know how long to spend trying to catch such a fish. Some fish will wake up and grab your fly after a number of casts, while others will pay it no attention. In general it is probably better to move to another fish sooner rather than later, particularly if another angler is fishing behind you. If you are fishing in the company of an experienced friend, he or she will suggest when it is time to move on. Even so, there are fish that can be caught but it can take a long time to work out just what they are feeding on before eventually selecting the right fly.

Fishing the water if there are no fish rising – or fish to be seen in a river – and there is nothing happening can be a good way to get your eye in

and build your level of concentration ready for when the fish do start to rise. However, some disapprove of fellow-anglers fishing the water instead of casting to a specific, visible or feeding fish, as they claim that it leaves little or no water untouched for an angler fishing behind. This is a point that is worth remembering if you are sharing a beat or stretch of water with one or more anglers.

You can make a virtue out of stopping to have your lunch if you have been trying to catch a fish for some time without success. Leaving the fish alone to have a rest while you eat will give it a chance to recover its confidence and, all being well, start feeding again

Jérôme Philipon

85

If you are wading, staying close to the bank will help break up your profile so you are not so obvious to fish. If you are very close to the bank on the side of your casting arm, it may be necessary to do an off-the-shoulder lift-off and cast as there won't be space between you and the bank

WADING

Although it can make sense to fish in waders, it does not follow that you should wade whenever possible. In fact it is better to wade as little as possible and wade only when essential or really necessary. When you are wading you have much

reduced vision upstream as you are closer to the water – although you are also less visible to fish compared to when standing on the bank.

Also, when wading, you have to move slowly and gently so that you make as little disturbance as possible. So having to move any distance to cover a fish that you spot further upstream will take longer than walking along the bank. While wading, look down at your waders regularly and you may see hatching or newly hatched flies crawling out of the water and up your waders. This shows you that it may be time to switch from fishing a nymph to an emerger or a dry fly, if you are not doing so already.

If you are thinking of wading, before getting into the river you need to be sure that the bottom is suitable and the water is not too deep. Wading may be banned on some rivers, restricted to certain areas, or unrestricted. If you don't know the river and are not with anyone who can give you any guidance, it is always better to err on the side of caution rather than risking a ducking or getting stuck. Unless the bank is very low and the water shallow, never try stepping off the bank into the river. It may look shallow, but very clear water is often much deeper than you appreciate.

There will be places, such as a cattle drink,

The appearance of flies on your waders may be the first indication that a hatch has started

that can work. Getting out of a river can be a challenge where the bank is high. The best way to do this is to put your rod on the bank well out of the way and then, making sure that you have got a good footing, get hold of the bank and pull yourself up and out of the water. Once out of the water and on your hands and knees, you can crawl to a safe place to stand up and then retrieve your rod.

SPOTTING

One of the most interesting things that the first-time angler can do – apart from catching that first fish – is to fish with a knowledgeable friend and take turns to watch what happens when casting to a fish that you can see clearly in the water. Is it taking any notice of your fly? Does it move and have a look? If it takes the fly, how far did it move? In order to do this you have to be very careful about getting into a suitable position to watch the action without frightening the fish. As the spotter you can learn a lot and, when you change positions, the spotter can give you advice on the accuracy of your casting and the placing of your fly. There is more information about this subject in the section on reading the water and seeing fish, later in this chapter (see page 91).

Left It can be easier to get into a river if you kneel down or even sit down and slide in slowly and carefully. Always check the depth of the water before getting in

where it is possible to walk straight into the river. Where the banks are high it may look ungainly, but sitting down and sliding gently into the water is better than trying to step in. Kneeling on the bank, with your back to the water, and putting one foot in at a time, is another approach

Getting out of the water can be easier if you put your rod down on the bank so you have both hands free. You can then pull yourself up the bank and out of the river

Fly choice

DRY FLY OR NYMPH?

It's worth remembering the Army maxim: 'Time spent in reconnaissance is seldom wasted.' Time spent observing what is happening – or not happening – will always pay dividends. So before tying-on a fly and making your first cast spend a minute or two looking around and at the river. Are there any flies hatching? Can you see any fish feeding– rising and taking flies on the surface of the water? Are they moving from side to side, feeding on nymphs below the surface? Swallows and swifts fly up and down over waters, feeding on flies on the water and in the air. Activity from these birds can often be the first sign that flies are hatching and that you should expect to see fish rising. These birds can appear, and then disappear just as suddenly, at almost any time of the day. The birds' activity, or lack of it, relates to the fact that hatches can start and stop, fish come on the feed (and start rising) and stop with seemingly no warning or obvious reason. Hatches can be more predictable and regular on some rivers and almost entirely unpredictable on others. The wind direction, air temperature and atmospheric pressure can all affect how the fish will behave and what sort of a day's fishing you have. Trout are affected by changeable weather and feed most actively when the weather is settled.

The season and time of day that you are fishing will help to determine whether to fish dry flies or nymphs. Are you fishing at a time of good hatches, for example in May or June when you might expect mayflies to be hatching? Have you a preference for keeping things simple and watching a dry fly, or do you prefer the challenge of fishing a nymph underwater? If there are fish rising and flies on the water then go for a dry fly. If there is little evidence of a hatch (of flies) and you can see fish feeding below the surface, then the correct and most productive way to fish will be with a nymph.

HOW TO SELECT A FLY

Once you have decided to fish a dry fly or a nymph, which actual fly do you choose? Although trout are speculative feeders, they can be selective in their choice of fly so it helps to have an

The higher above the water you can get the easier it will be to see fish. But if you stand too high and too close to the water you will frighten fish as they will be able to see you very easily

Although experienced anglers usually have boxes full of different patterns and sizes of flies, beginners should restrict their selection so that they can learn which ones work and which ones do not

understanding of what they are feeding on. Sometimes there will be plenty of flies in evidence – on the water or in the air – so it is then a case of selecting an artificial that is a good match for the size, shape and colour of the natural flies. This is what is known as 'matching the hatch'. But if there is no hatch to match, use a fly you like the look of, or one that has caught you a fish. In other words, one in which you have confidence.

The lists of recommended flies in this book include patterns that are designed to match and be good imitations of specific natural flies, while others are more general patterns that can be fished to represent a wide range of flies. The latter are good patterns to use when you are unsure

what the fish are taking and you want to search a piece of water in the hope of finding a feeding fish.

When you have decided what type of fly to use and selected one from your fly box, before you can attach it to your leader you need to add a tippet (if you have not done this already). A tippet should be about 4 ft (1.2 m) in length, unless it is a very windy day, when you should reduce the length by up to half. Pull off the required length of mono from the spool of tippet material, plus a bit more than the finished length so that you can tie your knots. If, as recommended, you have a little ring on the end of your leader, use a tucked half blood knot to attach the tippet. If you have a loop on the leader, tie a surgeon's

You can fish small flies with thinner tippets but big flies need a thicker tippet

tippet and fly regularly. If the tippet has one or more casting knots, change it straight away. Casting knots are one of the most likely reasons for a tippet breaking. And make sure to check that your fly is still tied on properly. Even experienced anglers can find that they have managed to wrap the tippet round the fly. You need to get into the habit of checking regularly for casting knots (especially on windy days) and also checking your hook to make sure that it still has got a point. A fly with a broken hook is great for getting fish to rise but you will never be able to catch them! Always check your tippet when you reel-in your line to move to another place, and each time you pause while fishing, such as when waiting for a fish to rise or show itself. All being well there will be no problems but, having made a check and rectified the problem, you can be confident that your tackle is not going to let you down.

The surgeon's loop is a quick and easy way to join lines together and to undo them when necessary

When you change fly always make sure that when you return it to its box you have not left any tippet material in the eye of the hook. You can waste valuable time changing flies when you have to clear the hook eye first

loop (see page 175) on the end of the tippet so that the two can be joined together using the loop-to-loop connection. This is a knotless method of joining together two pieces of line which have a loop on one end.

During the course of a day's fishing, each time that you change your fly you will reduce the length of tippet.

When using a short tippet on a windy day you may need to change it quite quickly but, in general, it is a good idea to put on a new one when you have about half the original length left. As well as changing your tippet once it starts getting too short, you must check your leader,

When first tying on a fly, or changing fly, make sure that you trim the tag end so that it is only about 2 mm long. If you leave it too long it may catch bits of weed floating on the surface or a fish may feel it and reject your fly

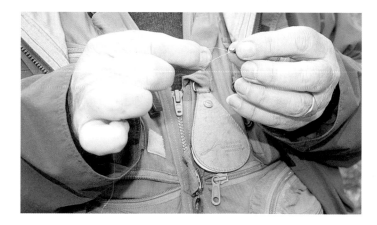

Reading the water and seeing fish

Reading the water is the process that you go through to try to find what you hope will be productive water where there are fish that you can cast to and, all being well, have a chance of catching. Part of the process of learning to read the water is to try to identify places where fish may be lying. Some parts of a river will have more suitable lies than others but, until you have some understanding of how to read the water, you may not know where the less-favourable areas are. The main requirements for a fish to prosper in a river are cover from predators, both overhead (cormorants for example) and in the river (pike, otters), somewhere to lie without using more energy than necessary and a good and regular supply of food. A fish needs to consume more energy than it uses if it is going to grow and put on weight, so it needs to spend most of its time out of the full force of the current. The biggest fish will use its size to take charge of the best lie, with fish in descending sizes occupying the less favourable spots. When a fish is caught or disappears, its place will often be taken by the next biggest. The beginner needs to fish as much water as possible in order to start building a mental picture and a store of knowledge of what good, fish-holding stretches of river look like. And, just as important, the less productive places, so that valuable time is not wasted fishing areas unlikely to hold a fish.

When you see a fish is it a happy fish or a frightened one? A fish swimming about undisturbed creates little or no disturbance itself. But when a fish is frightened – spooked by a clumsy approach or a bad cast – it will charge off, often leaving significant ripples or a wave on the surface, and sometimes a puff of sand or silt will rise from the riverbed as it accelerates away.

If you can see a fish, or a number of fish, in a river it makes trying to catch one a great deal easier. Some people have eyesight that is better suited to the task, and/or have better ability to spot fish in a river than others. But with the help of a good pair of polarized glasses you can train yourself to spot fish in a river. One of the most important things to remember when trying to see fish in the water, whether a river or a still-

water, is to look *through* the surface of the water, not just *at* it. It is often much easier to see fish in the river when you are actually fishing as you tend to look *into* the water rather than at it. The clarity of the water and the available light will, obviously, effect how easy it is to see fish. Chalk streams tend to have water that is gin clear so you can see every pebble on the riverbed, while rivers and streams running off peaty moorlands will have water tinted the colour of weak tea without any milk. Another problem is that trout can change their colouring to blend in with the riverbed: fish living over a sandy or chalky bottom will be much lighter in colour compared to fish living where the bed is covered in dark weed or rocks. The more time that you can spend looking *into* rivers, the better.

When the water is really clear and the light good, it is much easier to see fish compared to when the water is coloured and the light is bad

Trout are adept at changing their colouring so that they are less visible to their predators. When I took this photograph I hoped that the fish would be really easy to see as the water was so clear. But the fact that the trout are not easily distinguishable shows how well they disguise their presence. It is probably a good representation of what can be seen in most rivers

When standing or fishing on a high bank you must take extra care not to frighten the fish that may be able to see you

Sometimes a change of position can help: another angle and the light falling in a slightly different way can both be significant factors. It also helps to be as high as possible above the water – but do be careful not to make yourself so obvious to the fish that they all disappear in terror.

Conversely, when wading, because you are much closer to the water it is not so easy to see fish unless they are quite close to you. When you plan to wade, have a good look at the water from the bank before getting in and try to make a mental note of the position of likely target fish: is there a clump of weed close by, or a fence post, or tree branch? If you are standing with the sun behind you, make sure that your shadow does not fall on the water.

While a fish's *colour* may not be obvious in water, their *movements* can be – particularly those of their tail. A fish's movements can often be

noticed because they are not in sequence with the regular movement of a piece of weed, for example, that is moving continuously in the current. As well as moving continuously, a piece of weed will have a tapered end, whereas a trout's tail, which has quite a straight edge, may give the fish away by its shape, as well as by its varying movement. That said, even when you have some experience, it is still easy to cast to a piece of weed that looks just like a fish.

On sunny days it is often possible to spot a fish's shadow on the riverbed, particularly in clear shallow water with a sandy bottom. Also on sunny days you may spot a flash in the water as a fish turns to intercept a nymph. You may see something that does not look 'quite right' that is worth a second look and could turn out to be a fish. When there is broken cloud try to take advantage of the times when the sun is out to have a good look into the water, as you should be able to see more than when there are clouds overhead.

Spotting fish in broken water is more difficult, but even here you will find calm patches on the surface that you can look through more easily. And on windy days there will be lulls in the wind which allow a view below the surface. If you do not develop your fish-spotting skills and either fish blind or simply 'fish the water' in the hope of finding a fish, you risk 'lining' and frightening fish that you either cannot see or have not seen.

Knowing where to look for fish helps as well. As hinted at above, trout like what is sometimes known as 'structure' in a river so it makes sense for you to look for this. Examples of structure that attract fish are a stone or boulder, a depression in the riverbed, a tree trunk or branch that has fallen into the water – anything that deflects the full force of the current and provides a lie where a fish can 'hang out', where it has some protection from predators, has access to food, and does not have to use all its energy to stay in one place.

There is a section of a famous tributary of the River Test that flows through a straight concrete channel, with a flat bottom and vertical sides, for a few hundred yards through a watercress farm. It really is the most unlikely place to find wonderful wild trout, but live there they do. They are to be found by one or two water inlets, which are a source of food and well-oxygenated turbulent water; tucked into the corner between the walls and the bottom of the channel, and in places where there are pipes running along the walls. Each of these features provides cover and security in its own way.

On sunny days you may see the shadow cast by a fish before the fish itself

Overhanging branches provide valuable cover, and a source of food items such as falling caterpillars, for fish

Fish don't lie under bridges or overhanging branches because they know that it is difficult for an angler to cast a fly to them. They like these lies because there is overhead cover from predators, and because food items such as caterpillars will drop from trees and bushes into the river. When searching the water for a likely place to find a fish, deeper water is often darker than shallow water and may hold fish. Bends in a river and areas of deeper water may have eddies. (A fish lying in a back eddy may be facing downstream when compared to the main current but is, in fact, facing upstream into the flow of the back eddy.)

There are low-pressure areas even in the fastest and roughest of rivers where fish can rest out of the full strength of the current. If there are large stones and boulders in a river, look for fish lying in the low-pressure area *in front of* any such obstruction. Where there is a large boulder in a river, there is always a low-pressure area in front where the flow splits to pass either side of it. The roughness of the bed of a river slows the flow,

which is how and why fish spend a lot of time very close to the bottom where they are lying in a slacker current. You can see this for yourself by pushing a stick into a patch of sand or silt. This action will displace fine grains which will form a plume that drifts up towards the surface and then downstream as it reaches the surface and spreads out as it is swept along by the faster current. You will often see fish lying right on the bottom and if one proves to be very difficult to catch it is probably because it is asleep. Brown trout will sometimes sleep all day and only start to stir as night comes with the setting of the sun.

Variations in the speed and direction of surface currents can make the presentation of a dry fly difficult. These variations may pull at your leader and make your fly drag in an unnatural manner, or even result in your fly being swept past a feeding fish out of its vision. While this is obvious when fishing with a dry fly, it is disguised when fishing a nymph below the surface, but may have an equally harmful effect. Various

Jérôme Philipon

strategies can be used to reduce or overcome the problems caused by variations in current flow. A change of position might help reduce the number of variations in flow to be overcome, or casting so that there is extra slack in your line will give you a longer drift before drag sets in. A short cast with your rod held high to lift your line off the water may also help you avoid having your line pulled in the wrong direction. Let's look more closely at the question of presentation and line management.

The importance of good presentation and line management

One of the keys to successful fly fishing is good presentation of the angler's fly to a fish. A fly cast carefully and accurately to a place where a fish is expecting to see food items will often be rewarded with a rise. A good short cast will always be better than a poor long cast, and managing

your line (and rod) well will help you to make better casts and fish a cast well. It is too easy to make a presentable cast to a fish which then rises to your fly but, because you are having to organize the line in your hand and get things under control, you fail to set the hook and so fail to catch the fish. It can happen that a fish will seize your fly as it lands on the water and you need to be ready to set the hook quickly if this happens. You want to have your line under control at the end of the presentation cast so that you can start retrieving line straight away and keep in contact with your fly.

Part of doing this is knowing where your hands are, in relation to each other, your rod and line, so that you can take hold of the line with your line hand, or place it behind the index finger of your rod hand without looking.

When casting, you want a dry fly to touch down on the water as lightly as possible, creating as little disturbance as possible. However, trout can be very contrary and don't

Careful wading can help an angler get into a position where he, or she, can make a shorter, more accurate cast. On sunny days try to make sure that any shadow from your line will fall on the far side of a fish

Sometimes a fish will take your fly as it touches the water. You must always be ready for this to happen

Well-mown and very tidy banks may look nice but they are of little help in providing cover for fishermen

always do what you expect and there will be times when your fly hits the water with a splash and you catch a fish. This could be because the splash woke the fish, or it thought that something worth eating had landed on the river. So, although you should always try to ensure that your fly lands gently, don't be surprised if you rise a fish to a bad, splashy cast. Nymphs, particularly well-weighted ones, will make a bit of a splash as they hit the water. This can actually be very helpful as it shows you where your fly has landed.

Getting into the optimum position to cast to a fish or a rise, whether on the bank or wading, will allow you to make an *accurate* cast of a sensible length. There is rarely any need to make the longest cast that you can, but equally you do not want to get so close to a fish that you frighten it by your presence. You need to make a judgement about how close is too close. The clarity and depth of the water will both affect how well you can see a fish, and how well that fish can see you. If you get too close and frighten a fish, next time make sure that you keep a bit further away. Always try to make the best use of any bankside vegetation to disguise your presence. This will be difficult if you are fishing where the banks are mown almost to the river's edge. Keeping back from the edge of the bank and crouching down will also help you to get a little bit closer to a fish.

Sunny days, when the sun is high in the sky and the water gin clear, are ideal for seeing fish in the water, but can also make a great presentation very difficult. On a sunny day your rod may catch the sun and make a flash at just the wrong moment, or it or your line will, literally, cast a shadow over the water or on the riverbed that sends your target fish scurrying for cover. You can reduce the risk of rod flash by making the minimum of false casts and casting so that the line's shadow is as far from the fish as possible. If you cast on the sunny side of the fish then the shadow of the line will be that much closer to the fish and so more likely to frighten it.

If you choose to wade, once in the water and wading you must move slowly and carefully so you do not send great ripples out in front of you as you move upstream and perhaps clouds of sand and silt downstream. Both are caused by clumsy wading. As you take each step, always make sure that you can see where you are about to put your foot. In lowland rivers you might be about to step into a hole or a silty patch, while in rivers with rocky bottoms you could easily get your foot trapped between two rocks, or find yourself plunging into a deep hole that you had not seen. You might even step on an unstable boulder or rock and take a tumble. Always use a wading staff to support yourself and feel the bottom in anything but shallow and low-velocity rivers. Even in slower rivers if you would feel happier using a wading stick don't be embarrassed. And, if you find yourself off-balance and unsure of your next foothold, take care and, if necessary, back-track.

When you are happy that you are in the best position to cast to a fish, you will need to take into account the strength of the current and whether there are variations in the speed of flow between you and the fish that might cause problems such as making your fly drag. Sometimes the best cast will be upstream and at quite an acute angle to a fish; at other times a cast more or less straight across the river might be a better option.

Once you have made a cast you need to remove excess slack from the line so that you are in contact with your fly and so able to set your hook when a fish rises and takes it. On stillwaters you need to stay in contact with the fly, or flies, at the end of your line so that you can feel any gentle takes, but when fishing running water you must retrieve line all the time.

The basic requirement is to retrieve line at the same speed as the river is flowing, keeping in contact with your fly all the time, but without disturbing its natural drift. An exception to this can be if you are fishing a pattern designed to

represent egg laying caddis that are skittering and fluttering over the surface: this is one occasion when retrieving your artificial in short bursts so that it disturbs the surface can be very effective. Your aim should always be to retrieve line in a tidy and orderly way so that it doesn't get tangled up and you don't end up standing on your expensive fly line, and so you are ready to play a fish should one rise to your fly.

As you retrieve line try to keep it in neat coils in your line hand

The minute you stop retrieving and let your concentration wander is the minute when a fish will take your fly

Retrieving line involves both hands working in sequence. Pull with your line hand, then hold the line against the rod handle with your rod hand while you move your line hand along the line ready to recover more line

Good line management will enable you to make another cast quickly and efficiently. To retrieve line you must hold the line against the rod handle with the index finger of your rod hand while you pull it in with your line hand. Each time you move your line hand backwards to retrieve line, ease the pressure of your index finger. Then hold the line tight while you move your line hand back to your rod and take hold of the line again, by the rod handle. You will now have a loop of line in your line hand. Repeat this process as many times as necessary until it is time to lift your line and fly off the water to make another cast. There will be times when you will need to use your rod as well as your line hand to retrieve line. As your fly approaches the end of a drift you may want to leave a little more line on the water: you can do this by stopping retrieving line and, instead, raising your rod tip and using a roll cast to lift your line off the water and then make a false cast. Technically, the result is known as a combination cast, but don't let that concern you too much.

The final action with your line hand comes when you wind in your line, when you want to move to another spot, you want to have a rest, or at the end of the day when you stop fishing. As you wind line back onto the reel spool, apply some tension with your line hand and try to move

the line from side to side so that it winds on evenly. (If you have set up your reel to wind with your line hand, then you will use your rod hand to control the line.)

When moving from place to place or moving up the riverbank, hook your fly in the top guide (the one before the tip ring) and then loop your leader and line around the reel before reeling-in the slack line, instead of holding your rod and fly in one hand and coils of line in the other. If you do the latter, you will find that your line is in a tangle as soon as you want to make another cast. It may seem a time-wasting fiddle to reel-in your line as described but it is less time-consuming – and less frustrating – than removing knots from your fly line while a fish is rising close by. Not only does it prevent tangles but, because the end of your fly line and leader are outside the tip ring, it is very much easier to start casting again. When you are ready to cast again, unloop the line from around your reel and let the loop of line and leader hang out over the water. Now tap your rod smartly just above the handle and, all being well, the fly will jump out of the guide so that you can start casting. (This is one time when it is acceptable to poke your rod out over the water.)

Keeping your line under control as much as possible will benefit your time on the river as you

Tapping your rod firmly will disengage the fly from the guide. Now you can strip off some line and start casting

should have fewer tangles to frustrate you which will help you to catch and land more fish and make your line last longer. Fly lines don't like being stood on, particularly on stony or muddy ground.

Has that fish taken my fly?

When a fish rises and takes your fly, so that you can play it and then get it into your landing net, you need to set the hook in its mouth. But in the excitement of the moment it is all too easy to be too quick trying to set the hook and pull your fly out of a fish's mouth. A fish that has risen to a dry fly on the surface needs to be given enough time to take the fly and then turn down with the fly in its mouth before you raise your rod to set the hook. While it is obviously terribly disappointing and frustrating to get a fish to take your fly only to pull it straight out of its mouth, try not to worry too much, as even experienced anglers still make the mistake of trying to set the hook too quickly, or sometimes not quickly enough.

How will you know if a fish has taken your fly? If you are fishing a dry fly, as long as you are watching your fly (the moment you lose concentration and perhaps look away is the moment when a fish will rise to your fly), you should see

the fish rise up and take the fly into its mouth. Sometimes there will be a disturbance or swirl in the water by your fly. Some fish will rise to the surface slowly and sip-in your fly very gently, creating the minimum of disturbance. In complete contrast, another fish will hurl itself out of the water, perhaps with your fly in its mouth, or it will take your fly as it re-enters the river (or it may miss on the way up and on the way back). And if there are a lot of natural flies on the river, some will be close to your fly and you may see a fish rise to what you thought was your fly but find it has actually taken a natural fly close by. If you are not certain whether or not a fish has risen to your fly, perhaps because you can't see it clearly amidst a lot of naturals on the water, or the light is not very good, it is always worth raising your rod to set the hook just in case. If there is no fish there, be prepared to make another cast. If you are having trouble following your fly on the water, try casting a shorter line to keep your fly within easier view. Shorter casts will have the added benefit of improved accuracy.

(While it is generally fairly easy to know when a fish has risen to a dry fly, one of the real challenges of nymph fishing is knowing when a fish has taken your fly. We will look at this in detail in Chapter 8.)

To set the hook you raise your rod from pointing at the water (as you retrieve line) so that it is pointing towards the sky. While you do this – something that takes only a fraction of a second – you must keep the line trapped against the rod handle with the index finger of your rod hand and also hold the line firmly with your line hand. You may also need to pull in line to stop it going slack between you and your fish, or to give the fish some line if it wants to make a run. If you have too much slack line between you and your fly it can be difficult to tighten the line enough to set the hook firmly. But the action of a fish turning-down from the surface, with your fly in its mouth, will help the fish to partially hook itself.

Playing and netting a fish

Once you have set the hook you then have to play the fish. The process of playing a fish is designed to let it use up its energy so that you can bring it quickly to your net, either to release it and return it to the water, or to despatch it swiftly if you intend to take it home to eat. Very small fish can be netted quickly as they will not have enough strength to resist, but with a bigger fish more time and care must be taken and you will need to watch and concentrate on what the fish is doing.

Size isn't everything when it comes to how much of a struggle a fish will make to retain its freedom. A large, flabby stock fish will not put up much of a fight compared to a smaller, well-conditioned wild trout. Also, the strength of current in which fish live affects how strong they are. A fish that goes from a hatchery into deep, slow water will never develop the well-toned muscles of a wild fish living in a strong current. A funky wild fish feels like a piece of spring steel on the end of your line in comparison to the sometimes slower, boring runs of a stock fish.

It is all but impossible to explain to a beginner just how hard they can hold a fish or how much slack line to allow it. You can only find out by practical experience. Many small fish can be brought more or less straight to the net or bank, as discussed. An experienced, knowledgeable companion can see from the bend in your rod how hard you are having to hang on, can estimate the size of the fish and, being mindful of the type of water you are fishing, can advise how much line you should give, how quickly you can pull in slack line and when you should start to get ready to net something more substantial.

While playing a fish it is important to keep

Every angler, whether new to the sport or an experienced old hand, likes to see a good bend in their rod

your rod tip up and to keep tension on your line. If you let the line go slack the hook may fall out of the fish's mouth. Should you be fortunate enough to hook a fish bigger than you expect, you will need to hold the line firmly enough to keep the fish under control, but you must also be prepared to give it line so that it can make a run. You may see the fish and realize its size, or just be aware that it pulls hard. If you simply hang on to the line as tightly as you can, you risk the fish breaking the line or even the hook pulling free. If you find it difficult to hold your rod up and the fish is trying to pull the tip down to the water, that is a good indication that you should give the fish some line and let it make a run or two. When a fish makes a run you must be ready to retrieve line if it turns and comes back towards you. Inevitably there will be times when you hold a fish too hard and the tippet snaps and other times when you don't apply enough tension and the fish comes off. It's all part of the process of becoming a fly fisher.

In general, fish are played by holding the line in your line hand – rather than using the reel – so that you can feel what the fish is doing and release line quickly when necessary. With big fish, such as are to be caught in some stillwaters, it may be necessary to wind slack line onto your reel and play the fish using the reel. This will mean that you lose some sensitivity, but it does have the benefit of keeping your line off the ground and free from snags.

Always try to keep downstream from a fish so that the fish will be fighting you and the current. If a fish gets below you, you are then playing the fish against the current and are much more likely to lose it. When it tires you will have to pull it back up to you against the current. As well as swimming up, across or down the river, fish will seek refuge in obstacles such as weed beds and tree roots. You can use side strain to keep fish away from a hazard. As the name suggests, side strain means pulling the fish with your rod angled to one side or the other, depending on which way you want to steer the fish. Side strain also helps to disorientate a fish.

One of the main problems to worry about when playing a fish whilst you are wading can be stopping it from dashing between your legs and possibly taking a complete turn around one or both legs! It can be difficult to get out of the way quickly enough to prevent this from happening. It is important to get the fish under control – and keep it under control – as quickly as possible. When you are in the water it is more of a

A wonderful wild brown trout is returned to the river where, all being well, it will continue to grow and put on weight

challenge to follow a lusty fish that makes a deter-mined run for freedom – if you are on the bank you can always run after it – and so you may need to be prepared to give it more line. Be ready to gather in slack line when a fish turns and runs towards you. But one advantage of being in the water is that it should be easier to see any poten-tial underwater snags that the fish may aim for in an attempt to free itself from the restraint of your hook and line. Whether playing a fish from the bank or in the water, do try to keep it in sight all the time.

Try not to play a fish for any longer than you have to, particularly if you intend to release it. Playing a fish creates lactic acid in its muscles and the greater the build-up of lactic acid the longer it will take the fish to recover. Also, playing a fish

You should always try to net a fish as quickly as you can so that you do not make the fish over-exert itself

longer than necessary increases the chance of losing it as the hook-hold may be weakened. Once a fish starts to make fewer and shorter runs or starts to turn onto its side, then you can get ready to net it. If you have a net with a fixed frame make sure that it is to hand; if you have a folding net, unfold it ready for action. There is only one thing more upsetting than losing a fish while you are playing it and that is losing it just as you are about to net it.

Don't wave your net around as doing so may frighten the fish into making a last lunge for freedom. This is crucial if you have got the join between your fly line and leader inside the top ring of your rod. If a fish makes a last dash and the line catches in the top ring, you will probably lose it when the tippet breaks. So always be prepared when you have got to this stage and be ready to give a little line if necessary. The best way to net a fish is to lower your net into the water and then draw the fish over it. Once it is over the net, lift the net and fish up quickly out of the water. Try not to keep lunging at a fish with your net as this will frighten it.

Jérôme Philipon

Jérôme Philipon

When netting a fish try to keep your net in the water and draw the fish over it. When the fish is in the net you can lift it out of the water

If you have caught a small fish it is usually possible to guide it close enough to you so that you can reach down and take hold of the tippet, then slide your hand down it and grasp the fly in your finger and thumb. Hold the fly firmly and either give it a push and twist to free it, or let the fish kick itself free. While you are doing this you will have to hold your rod out of the way, but be prepared to use it to play the fish if you fail to keep hold of the hook. If the hook is not immediately accessible with your fingers, take hold of it carefully with your forceps and remove it quickly. All being well you will have released the fish without actually having to handle it.

It is good practice to net bigger fish. Once you have your fish in the net, tuck the butt of your rod under your armpit or, if you are close to the bank, you may be able to rest your rod on the bank or some bankside vegetation. Hold the fish in the net as the net itself will help you to hold it without having to grip it too tightly. After you have unhooked it, you will probably need to cradle it in the water, facing into the current, while it recovers its breath before you release it. Should you let a fish go too quickly and it sinks to the bottom, or turns on its side, try to net it again so that you can hold it for a bit longer until it is strong enough to kick itself free and swim off.

Regardless of whether you are on the bank or in the water, whilst being played, some fish will bore deep while others will run and jump clear of the water, which adds to the excitement. If a fish does jump or rolls and turns in the water, it can happen that the tippet gets wrapped around the fish. When this happens it may take a moment or two after netting it to work out where the tippet has gone before you can unravel it and release the fish. Another thing that will happen from time to time is your fly getting caught in the mesh of your net. Leave it alone until you have either released your fish or despatched it quickly. Never try to free a fly before dealing with a fish.

If you are going to keep a fish for the table, show it the respect it deserves and tap it firmly a couple of times on the back of the head with a priest.

Tim Gaunt-Baker

Only lift your net out of the water once you are sure that the fish is safely ensconced by it. There will be times when you need a landing net with a reasonable length of handle to be able to reach a fish from the bank. Tennis racket-style nets are popular but are restricted in where they can be used

A priest is the proper thing to use to kill a fish, not a piece of stick or landing net handle

When you intend to return a fish to the river handle it as little as possible and, if possible, unhook it as mentioned while it is still in the water. If you have to hold your fish while you unhook it, the easiest way to keep it still is to turn it over and hold it upside down. If you do this you will find that the fish will stay quite still. Fishing with barbless hooks, or hooks with the barb flattened, makes unhooking and releasing fish quick and easy. Try not to hold a fish too hard as you risk damaging its internal organs. You may, however, need to hold a fish firmly but gently, to stop it escaping from your hand as you remove the hook. One disadvantage of not netting a fish is that if it is very tired after you have unhooked it, it may sink to the bottom or be swept downstream before it can recover. If you net your fish, you can hold them in the water until they have recovered and swim away.

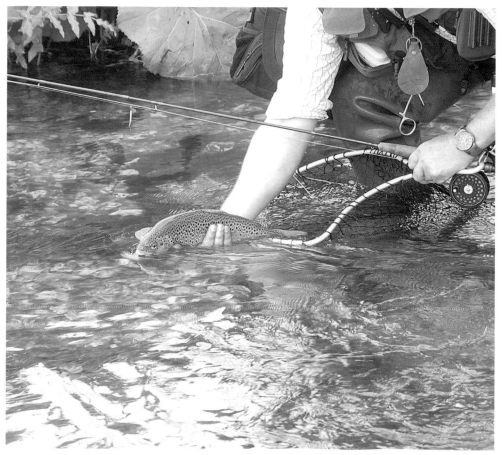

When holding a fish as you release it try not to grip it too tightly as you may damage its insides

Some fish will swim off before you have a chance to hold them while they recover. Others will appreciate some care and attention.

Fish will not always be hooked in the lip or the corner of the mouth, known as the scissors, where the fly can be removed quickly and easily. If a fish is hooked well inside its mouth, rather than trying to remove the hook with your fingers, use a pair of forceps to take hold of the fly and tweak it free.

Photographing fish

The time will come when you want to take a photograph of a fish that you have just caught. Now that digital cameras are ubiquitous, on a mobile phone, in compact form, or digital SLR, taking photographs has never been easier. In order to take a good photograph of a trophy fish, and do so in a way that will cause the least distress to the fish (if it is going to be released), you need to be able to do it as quickly as possible and it helps to have a companion to take the actual photograph. Keep the fish in the water until you are ready and then raise it out of the water as little as possible for the shortest time. This is the least harmful way to treat a fish. Some of the best photographs of fish are where they are half out of the water with their head pointing down towards the water rather than being held up, clear of the water, for everyone to see.

A very good South African angler and photographer, Tom Sutcliffe, has this advice for taking photographs of live fish out of water: 'Always hold your breath when you take pictures of fish out of the water. It will remind you when to submerge the fish to let it breathe [again].'

Lift a fish just high enough so that you can see its shape and wonderful colours

CHAPTER SEVEN

Fishing on the surface: dry-fly fishing

Casting a dry fly to a fish that can be seen rising to flies floating on the surface of a river is for many anglers the highest form of fly fishing

Presenting, with a graceful, effortless cast, a beautifully tied, realistic imitation of the flies floating down a river, as every now and then one or more disappears in the rings created by a trout as it rises – this is what even those with little or no knowledge of, or interest in, the sport consider to be fly fishing. Also essential to the scene are a warm and sunny day, a light breeze, birds flying up and down the river snatching flies as they take off, and banksides covered in lush vegetation and wild flowers. Although this may seem to be an idealized setting, there are still places where it is the reality.

Is the key to successful dry-fly fishing what is often known as 'matching the hatch', or presentation? I can still remember the time when I spotted a nice fish rising quite frequently close to the far bank of the river. I had a fly in my box that I had never used – it was an outlandish artificial butterfly with yellow foam wings – but something made me give it a try. I nipped off the fly that I had been using and tied on the yellow-winged butterfly. I cast over to the far bank and the fly landed gently just the right distance of a couple of feet upstream of its intended target. The fly drifted gently down and as it came into view, the fish rose up underneath it and swam gently round it in a complete circle before opening its mouth and taking the fly.

I am not sure whether I or the fish was more embarrassed when I was able to release it a

A trout caught on a dry fly; a little less garish than the yellow-winged butterfly

Tim Gaunt-Baker

minute or two later. Obviously my presentation was good, because my fly arrived just where the fish was expecting to see another fly, but there was no attempt at imitating anything likely to be seen on the river either that day or any time during the season. The fish gave my fly the closest inspection I have witnessed and still decided that it liked what it had seen.

Selecting a fly

Before tying a fly on to the end of your tippet you need to have some idea of which one to select. A few minutes spent quietly on the bank watching the water will be helpful. If there are flies – duns or caddis – on the water and you don't know their name, or names (and quite probably don't know the names of the flies in your fly box), then you should simply select an artificial that is similar in size, shape and colour to those on the water. This is the essence of trying to 'match the hatch'. There are anglers who will take this concept to what might seem ridIculous, obsessive lengths compared to those who believe that a generic artificial fly placed skilfully where a fish is expecting to see a fly is all that is needed. That is the basic concept of the importance of presenta-

tion. The hatch-matcher will have boxes full of artificial flies, in various sizes, tied to represent a wide range of flies and every stage in which they might be found.

The believer in presentation will carry relatively few patterns and will spend – compared to the 'hatch-matcher' – much less time agonizing about which pattern to select and whether it is the right choice. Fortunately neither approach will always be right – equally neither always wrong – and they will be a constant source of much discussion and argument over a glass of wine or pint of beer in a riverside pub.

And there will be times when using an artificial smaller than the natural can be very effective. A good example of this is when mayfly are hatching. A natural mayfly is a very large fly and artificials are often tied on hooks size 10 or even 8 (the lower the number the bigger the hook). But a pattern tied on a size 12 or even 14 hook may be very much more effective. Using the guidelines just mentioned, select what you think is the best choice of fly and make sure that your presentation is always as good as you can make it. Having some idea of what flies are likely to be in evidence, depending on the time of year when you are fishing, will help too. You are trying to

When you change flies always make sure that you put the discarded one back in the right fly box

select and present a fly to a fish that will think your fly is a food item, if it has the right trigger points, which are worth repeating: size and shape. There will be times when fish are feeding selectively, for example, choosing one natural fly rather than another (if more than one species is hatching), or feeding on a specific stage of a fly's life such as hatching flies, cripples or stillborns. They may ignore the most obvious fly in favour of something less visible or easy to spot.

Fish like feeding on hatching flies, or emergers, as they are an easy meal. Cripples and stillborns and flies struggling to escape their nymphal shuck quite often get stuck in the surface film where they have no means of escaping the jaws of hungry fish. For a fish this is an opportunity to get maximum energy input in return for minimum energy outlay. Although this chapter is all about *dry*-fly fishing, when you are fishing an emerger or spent pattern, you may actually want your fly to be a little damp, if not actually wet, so that it fishes in the surface film. There will also be times when it seems that a fish is attracted by the movement of a fly that suggests to the fish that it is alive. A gentle tweak on your line may be enough to give your fly a little twitch that will catch a fish's attention. This is something subtly different from a dragging fly, which is usually a real turn-off. This is worth trying if fish ignore a floating fly that is doing just that, without any movement.

While the majority of flies of interest to trout and trout fishermen are aquatic and hatch in or by water, trout will, as explained earlier, also feed on terrestrials (land-based insects) such as daddy-long-legs, grasshoppers, beetles and hawthorns that get blown onto the water at certain times of the year. A day when there are plenty of hawthorns in the air and a strong wind blowing them onto the water can produce spectacular fishing. Hawthorns have long dangly legs and are not strong fliers and once on the water they are helpless, as they cannot take off from an alien environment. Hawthorns and daddy-long-legs are easy to see in the air, on bankside vegetation and on the water. Sometimes you will see regular rises quite close to the bank and seemingly no flies to be seen. If this is happening it is worth searching through the vegetation, where you may well discover hundreds of little beetles, sometimes with dark green metallic-looking wings. These little beetles fall onto the water where they are consumed with relish by hungry fish.

Although in real life a mayfly is a big fly, it can often be much more effective to fish with an artificial that is quite a bit smaller

Dry flies that every angler should have, from left: Grey Wulff, klinkhåmer, black gnat and humpy

Some more essential dry flies: Griffith's gnat, elk hair caddis, Adams, parachute Adams and 'F' fly

If you end up 'fishing the water' because there are no fish to be seen rising, then a good general attractor pattern such as a humpy can be a very good choice. It is a fly that can represent everything and anything and provides a decent snack for a trout on the lookout for something to ease its hunger. If all else fails a little black fly – a black gnat for example – can often be a real killer.

Preparing for action

Once you have selected your artificial fly and tied it to the end of your tippet (using the Eugene bend) you will then need to apply some floatant to keep it dry and to prevent it from absorbing water. Doing this is a very good case of 'less is more'. If you apply too much of a paste-type floatant, instead of making the fly float higher and longer, what happens is that the hackles all get clogged and stuck together, the fly loses its vitality and ends up sinking. You can always add a little more floatant should you need to. When you have finished treating your

fly, if you have some floatant left on your fingers apply it to your leader or even the end of your fly line rather than simply wiping it off your fingers. When you grease your leader and tippet, don't grease the tippet closer than about 1 ft (30 cm) from the fly. The reason for this is that any grease on the tippet close to the fly will make it too obvious to fish. However, if you leave the whole length of the tippet ungreased, if it then sinks it may drag your fly underwater when you retrieve your line to cast again. You can also drown your fly if you are clumsy or try to retrieve it too quickly. When dry-fly fishing you do want to keep your fly as dry as possible. Keeping your fly dry will help reduce the number of false casts needed to dry it.

Dry flies do eventually get too wet and soggy to float, particularly if you have caught one or two fish with the fly and it has got some fish slime on it. Some days you will get minnows and other small fry nipping at your fly and occasionally pulling it under and drowning it, which is annoying. You can revive such a fly by giving it a

*When tying on a fly
make sure that you tie
the knot properly and
always moisten it with
some spit before
drawing it tight*

Jérôme Philipon

*Always be sparing when
applying floatant to a
dry fly*

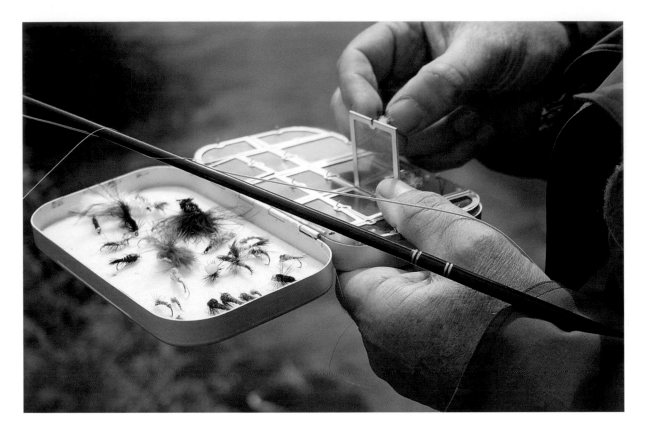

When a dry fly is really wet and soggy – after catching a number of fish, for example – it will be better to change it for a fresh, dry one

good wash in the water, blowing on it vigorously, drying it with a handkerchief, or subjecting it to a number of false casts, or a combination of these actions. When you are sure that it is really dry, apply a little floatant. Sometimes, though, however well you clean and dry a fly, it will simply refuse to stay afloat. As applying floatant to a wet and soggy fly does not work, the only remedy is to change to a new, clean and dry fly.

The approach and presentation

It took me a number of years to realize that a rising fish is not always where you think it is. Fish may often look up and see a fly on the surface floating towards them. As the fly floats downstream, the fish will rise up in the water and float downstream at the same pace as the fly, eyeing it up before rising to the surface and taking it. The fish, with the fly in its mouth, will then turn down and make its way back upstream to its regular holding spot. If the water is very clear you may be

able to see this happen. So, if you simply cast at the rings made by the rising fish, you will not actually cast to where the fish is, nor will you be casting to where the fish rose and took the fly. By the time the rise has registered on your brain, the rings will have travelled a little way downstream and if the fish has followed the fly before taking it, when it returns upstream it will be quite some way upstream from where you first thought you saw it rise. This means that instead of casting where you *think* the fish rose – and in reality behind or downstream of it – you must cast quite some distance *upstream* to stand any chance of your fly falling on the water in front of the fish where it can be seen. To have any chance of catching a fish you *must* cast, or present, your fly so that the fish can see it.

There is little to be gained by making the longest cast that you can to a fish. Doing this you risk losing accuracy, make it more difficult to see your fly (and this will be worse if there are a lot of naturals on the water), and make it more

Jérôme Philipon

difficult to set the hook should a fish rise and take your fly. But if you take the opposite approach and get too close to a fish, you will probably frighten it as soon as you start casting and the fish sees your rod and line waving around in the air above. It's a question of balance. The ideal position from which to cast to a feeding fish is close enough so that you can cast gently and accurately and you are concealed, whenever possible, so that the fish can't see you straight away. Try to make use of bankside vegetation and cover so that you are less obvious to fish in the water.

Although some river-keepers will mow the banks right to the edge of the water, the best banks have a nice thick cover of waist-high vegetation overhanging the river. This provides cover for the angler and fish as well as a source of food. If you stand behind such cover, it will break up your outline to about waist-height but if you kneel down, you will reduce your profile to a minimum.

Wild fish in clear, shallow water are easily scared so anglers need to make as much use as possible of bankside cover by keeping close to the bank when wading. There is a rhythm to fly fishing – cast and retrieve – which gives it a pleasing simplicity although the actual detail can be quite complex

Kneeling down and reducing your profile will help you get a little closer to wary fish

The speed of flow and depth of water will both play a role in how accurate you need to be when casting. Slow waters give fish far more time to see what is coming towards them compared to fast rivers and streams, where split-second judgements have to be made whether to take a fly or not. If a fish takes too long making up its mind, the fly will be gone. A fish lying in deep water has a wider field of view than one very near the surface, so it will be able to see flies further away from it. A fish near the surface in fast water may well not be able to see your fly if it passes by even a short distance away. All this means that you can cast closer to a fish in slow water, but in a fast river you will have to land your fly further away so that the fish has a chance to see it approaching before it disappears.

Always try to keep the end of your fly line away from or out of sight of the fish that you are trying to catch. Although it will not always be possible, do try to get into a position from where you can present your fly to the fish in a way that reduces the chance of it seeing and being frightened by your line. When you make a cast that results in the fly not landing where you had hoped it would, but is otherwise a respectable one, it is always worth fishing it out as you may find that there is another fish that you have not seen waiting for your fly to appear. If, instead of fishing the cast, you simply lift-off and cast again, the very act of lifting-off may frighten a fish that then spooks the one that you are trying to catch.

Although you will be able to see flies on the water much of the time when fish are actually rising and feeding on the surface, as was noted earlier, the fish may not be feeding on the most obvious or most numerous flies. They could be feeding selectively on something smaller that is less easy to see, or they could be feeding on nymphs that are hatching into adult flies. If a well-presented fly is refused, stop fishing and spend a few minutes observing what is happening. If

As you gain experience it becomes easier to judge how close to a fish you can and need to place your fly

there is a bush or some tall vegetation on the bank that you can hide behind close to the water, take advantage of it to get a closer and better look at the water.

When you are fishing nymphs (see next chapter) you need to eliminate virtually all the slack in the line between your rod hand and the fly (so you can set the hook quickly) but, in contrast, when dry-fly fishing you need a degree of slack line to prevent or delay the onset of drag from ruining a drag-free drift. Thus while the nymph fisher wants to cast a straight line, the dry-fly fisher is much happier with a nice wavy line on the water. And there are special, advanced casts designed to put slack into the line to help delay the onset of drag. Drag is caused by differences in the speed and direction of the surface flow of a river; by small currents generated by, for example, underwater features, and by retrieving line faster than the flow of the river. Sometimes these causes can be seen quite easily; at other times they will be a surprise. It is quite rare for the speed and direction of flow to be uniform across the width of a river, or up- and downstream. Some variations will be insignificant and can be ignored, while others will be sufficient to cause problems that need overcoming. Careful observation before casting and then considering the best position from which to do so to minimize the chances of drag ruining your cast will help.

MENDING THE LINE

There is a very useful line management technique known as mending your line. Knowing how to do this will, in certain circumstances, enable you to get a better or longer drag-free drift. Mending your line is when you use your rod to flip or move the line on the water surface, often in an upstream curve, to achieve a drag-free drift, or in such a way that a drag-free drift can be extended by combating the vagaries of contrary surface currents. If the variations in current are pulling your line downstream and creating a belly in it, this can be countered with an upstream mend. The more you have to cast across a river, rather than upstream, the more problems the variations in current will cause.

Making a mend is sometimes easier said than done, even though the technique is very simple. If you can see obvious variations in the current, you may want to make an upstream mend straight away rather than allowing the line to belly downstream. To make the mend you need to use the tip of your rod to first lift the line off the water and then flip or roll the section of the line that has created the downstream belly back upstream. You want to make a mirror image with your line. Lifting the line off the water breaks the surface tension while the line still on the water is held by the surface tension. Mending is easier to do the more line you have on the water. When you have perhaps only three, or even just two, rod-lengths of line out, if you are too aggressive you will pull on your fly, which you do not want to do as you want it to remain undisturbed. If you don't mend enough line, the current will still cause the line to drag your fly and, should you mend too much line, you can pull your fly away from the trout's feeding lane.

As well as making upstream mends, there will be times when, because your fly is coming downstream faster than your line, you will need to make a downstream mend to get fly, leader and line in the right order. From time to time you may have to make more than one mend, or even a number of mends through the duration of a cast, but do not get into the habit of mending the line for the sake of it: it won't help you catch more fish.

FISH CLOSE TO THE BANK

Fish that are lying and feeding very close to the bank will often present an interesting challenge. This is a good place to emphasize the importance of always fishing – by fishing I mean casting – very close to the bank, particularly when there is plenty of bankside vegetation overhanging the water. It is just as important to fish close in with a nymph as with a dry fly. Fish like the overhead security provided by the vegetation hanging over the water. They can tuck themselves in underneath where they are out of sight from flying predators and not too obvious to anything in the river, but where they can still spot flies coming downstream or that fall from the vegetation.

Many fish will lie and feed very close to the bank, perhaps within 6 in (15 cm), because they feel safe

To tackle such fish, first you will need to consider your angle of attack and the best position from which to cast. Finding that position will depend on the form of the bank and which bank the fish is lying under: the bank you are standing on or the other side of the river. If the fish is close to your bank and the bank is more or less straight, you may need to get into the river to give yourself an angle of attack. But if there is a bend or bulge in the bank between you and the fish, it may then be possible to cast straight upstream so that your fly lands on the water but some (or possibly most) of your line is on the bank, in effect a cross-country cast. This approach is good if you get the fish first cast, but if you don't tempt the fish to rise, you will need to be careful when you retrieve your line to make another cast, as you could end up hooking the bank or some vegetation. If this does happen, don't simply yank or tug your line as all you may

achieve is to drive the point of the hook further into what you have caught. Conversely, a gentle tweak may free your fly and cause it to drop onto the water again. If it doesn't come free, you will have to creep along the bank and free it by hand, all the while being as careful as possible not to be seen by any fish.

As long as the far bank is not too far away – that is within sensible casting range – getting your fly to the fish should be relatively easy. All being well you will be able to cast more across the river than the normal 'up and across' cast. But you will need to judge the length of your cast carefully so that your fly does not land on the opposite bank. If it does, don't do anything hasty! Take up any slack in the line – this action might be enough to free your fly – and then give it a very gentle pull. If things go your way, the fly will come free and drop delicately onto the water, right by the nose of a waiting fish. Although your

fly landing on the bank, or overhanging vegetation, will happen by mistake, there will be times when it is the very best way to seduce a fish into taking your fly. Don't cast your fly at the bank too hard as you do not want to lose it in the vegetation, and give it only a gentle tweak after it has landed. This is a tactic than can work well when terrestrials such as crane flies and grasshoppers and even beetles are about, as they will often either fall or be blown onto the water, sometimes with a plop. Trout can't resist them!

The evening rise

Fishing an evening rise on a still and balmy summer's evening can sometimes provide a spell of wonderful fishing. But an evening rise can be so short in duration that it is over almost before you have realized what was happening, which causes great disappointment and frustration. The evening rise will set the angler various challenges which have to be overcome to ensure any sport. Working out what the fish are feeding on is one challenge. Fast-fading light just as things really get started is another – which leads to the problem of changing flies. To help with the last point a small torch will be very useful but, when you use it, hold it in your teeth unless you were born with three hands – and do turn away from the water so that its light won't frighten the fish.

Fish could be feeding on egg-laying spinners, spent flies that are dead or dying after mating and egg-laying, or hatching nymphs or emerging caddis. Careful observation of what flies are in the air or on the water should give you some pointers, as may the rise-forms of feeding fish. If there is a significant hatch in progress, with a lot of flies on the water, as the light fades it will be increasingly difficult to see your fly on the water. It will help if you keep your casts short and

If casting to a fish rising under the tree on the far bank, you may need to guide your line and fly around the exposed weed, or be prepared to lift-off and cast again sooner than you'd like. This is to avoid your line getting impeded by the weed and perhaps making your fly drag

A really good evening rise is something to delight in if you happen to be on the river in the right place and at the right time. Evening rises are not as common or as long-lasting as they once were

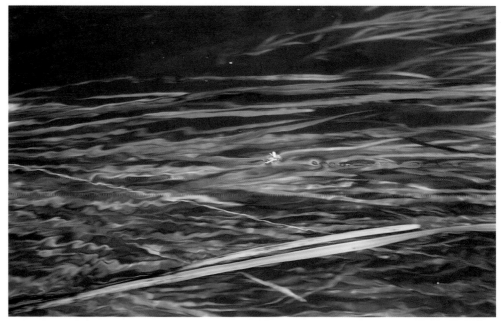

Parachute flies have a hackle tied horizontally around a coloured wing post. They float low in the water and the wing post can make them easier to see than some conventional dry flies

always raise your rod tip in anticipation of having hooked a fish whenever there is a rise where, or close to where, you think/hope your fly is. It can also help to fish a fly that has got either a white or black wing, or wing post in the case of parachute flies. It may seem counter-intuitive to use a black fly in fading light but it can sometimes be seen more easily.

Once again, accurate casting will help you to find your fly on the surface as the light fades, as you can concentrate on looking for it in the area where you intended it to land. You can also follow your line from the tip of your rod across the water (doing this can help you find a very small fly on the water even in good light).

Problem-solving

A problem that you can face when fishing the dry fly is seeing a fish that you are quite sure is rising to flies on the surface, but you cover it with a dry fly to no obvious effect.

If, after a number of good presentations – fly landing in the right place, no splashes from leader or line – you have not caught the fish or even risen it, what can be happening is that the fish is feeding just below the surface and what

When dry-fly fishing it helps to use a fly that you can see easily

Not every fish that leaves rise rings on the surface as it feeds is actually feeding on flies floating down the river. They can often be feeding on hatching nymphs or emerging flies

Instead of rushing to cast to a fish that you can see feeding, there will be times when it pays to slow down and spend a little time watching what is happening in and over the water

you are seeing are not rises to flies on the surface but sub-surface 'rises'. These are also known as 'bulgers' and are made by fish feeding on nymphs, or hatching nymphs which are also known as emergers. One approach to solving this problem is to try a different size of fly: generally small is the way to go. If this has no positive effect, try to work out what is happening by fishing artificials representing different stages in the life-cycle of a fly: sub-surface nymph, emerger or stillborns.

Although trout in stillwaters spend most of their time cruising around in search of food – because there is often little or no current to bring the food to them – there will be times when trout in rivers will cruise up and down a

particular stretch, rather than staying in one place waiting for the food to come to them. Cruising trout can be frustrating to catch as they move as you cast, but when you do connect with one the sense of achievement overcomes any frustrations. In a similar way to how a fish feeding very close to the surface will ignore your fly, with a cruiser when you cast to where you think it is, or should be, and you do not manage to rise it, it may have moved upstream or, if it was at the end of its beat, it could have gone back downstream. If you suspect that you are trying to catch such a fish, take some time to watch what it is doing. If there is a reasonable hatch of flies coming down the river, cruising fish can rise in a very rhythmical and regular pattern, picking

off a fly every few feet or so. Once you have established a rise pattern and got some idea of the fish's territory, you should be able to aim your cast so that your fly will be in the area where the fish will rise next.

There can be times when a fish will seize your fly the second it touches the water – which may happen for various reasons. Is it because your fly has landed in exactly the right place? Has it taken the fish by surprise? Or was the fish feeding on flies that were showing life by moving slightly perhaps to dry their wings? However, there will be times when it pays not to let a fish see your fly. You can do this by casting so that your fly lands on its nose. One time when this can pay is during a very heavy hatch where there are lots of flies on the water, or a significant number are being swept downstream in a feeding lane a bit like a conveyor belt. There are times when a fish will only take flies that move slightly, signalling to the fish that they are alive. If you suspect that this is happening try giving your line a slight tweak, so imparting a little movement to your fly. As mentioned earlier, moving a fly intentionally is not the same as a dragging fly, which is usually not helpful. But one time when drag can be productive is fishing a caddis, or sedge, when there are adults rushing about on the surface, and either allowing, or making, your fly drag is what the fish want.

Infrequent risers, often referred to as 'oncers', can also be a source of frustration. These fish can be very difficult to catch, either because they are not where you think they are or they are most probably not that hungry and so only consent to rise when something really juicy catches their eye. Perseverance will sometimes pay, making a number of casts all around the area where you think the fish is and casting well upstream. If it doesn't, move on in the hope of spotting a fish rising regularly.

One final point: do resist the temptation to go back downstream to cast to a fish that has started to rise, or keeps rising, after you have made your way upstream and past it. You can waste an awful lot of time gathering in your fly line, creeping back down the bank while trying to keep out of sight of the fish, turning round and then starting to cast. The only time that it is perhaps worth trying this is if you have fished all day, without success, and you are desperate to catch a fish before leaving the water.

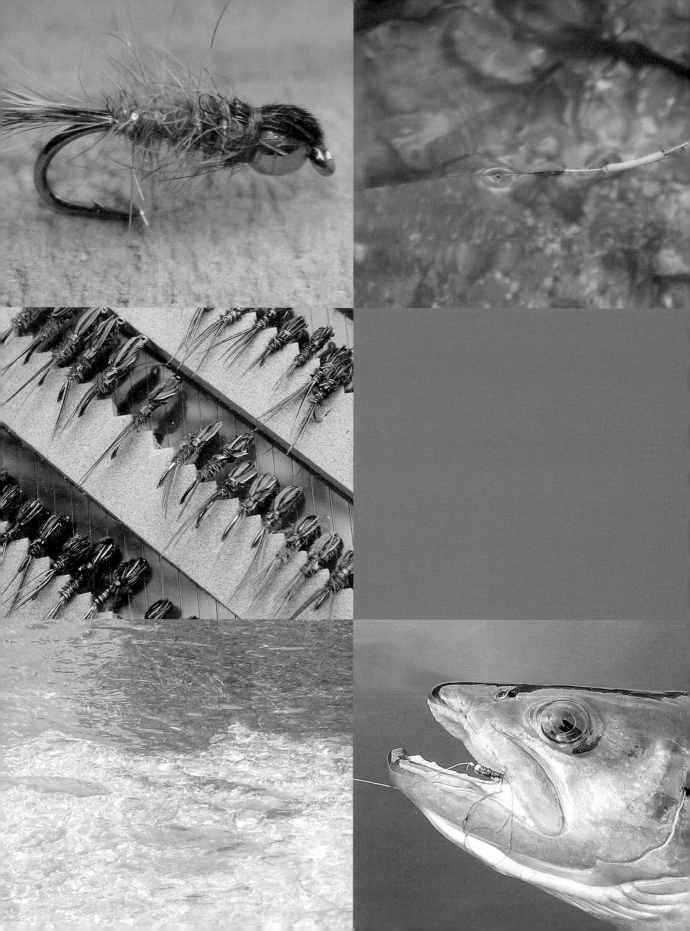

CHAPTER EIGHT

Fishing below the surface: nymph fishing

Nymph fishing is trying to represent a nymph swimming to the surface to hatch into a fly. The general shape, colour and size of an artificial nymph are more important than trying to fish an exact copy of natural nymphs.

A surprising number of otherwise experienced and competent fly anglers rarely, if ever, fish below the surface with nymphs. Various excuses are made, including a preference for seeing a fish rise and take a fly on the surface, or that they cannot see fish underwater. But these are excuses for the fact that they do not understand what they are meant to be doing. They don't know what is going on underwater and why they should be fishing there. One way to define a successful fly fisher is a person who fishes his or her fly at the level at which the fish are feeding. This could be fishing a dry fly on the surface as discussed in the previous chapter, or below the surface to fish feeding on nymphs. Certainly, for many anglers, the epitome of fly fishing is casting a dry fly to a rising trout feeding on hatching flies on the surface. But to ignore fish feeding below the surface is to deny many opportunities for exciting and challenging sport. Nymph fishing is both challenging and exciting; it can be difficult, but it is not impossible.

Catching fish that are feeding on nymphs below the surface presents real challenges for the newcomer to fly fishing. But once the challenges are understood, the rewards are real

Fishing an upstream nymph is fishing in three dimensions – one more than dry-fly fishing – as it involves judging how far upstream, in front of a fish, to cast; whether to cast to one side or the other, rather than straight over a fish; and, most important, how *deep* to fish your fly. As with dry-fly fishing, you can 'fish the water', but nymph fishing is made easier when you can make accurate casts to a fish that you can see feeding.

How do you know if a fish is feeding on nymphs? Key give-aways are how close to the surface the fish is, whether it is moving about in the water and whether you can see a flash of the white inside of its mouth as it takes a swimming nymph. Fish will sometimes be doing what is known as 'bulging' when taking nymphs in or just below the surface: you will often be able to see a bulge in the surface of the river that gives away their position, or you may see a dorsal fin or tip of the tail poking out of the water. Fish will feed very actively on nymphs at the start of a hatch and some will continue to take nymphs and hatching flies even when there are flies on the surface that have hatched. A bulge or sub-surface rise can be confused with that of a rise to a fly on the surface, but if you cast a dry fly to what is actually a sub-surface rise, do not be surprised when your fly is refused or ignored.

Although it is always advisable to wear polarized glasses when fishing, when nymph fishing their use is almost obligatory as they will help you to spot fish in the water, to see their reactions to your nymph and whether or not one takes your fly. As discussed in Chapter 6, developing the ability to see fish in the water is very important and will often contribute to a day's success.

Accurate casting

Although all methods of fly fishing require good presentation and accurate casting, it is even more important when fishing an upstream nymph. Sometimes a fish feeding actively will move a couple of feet or so to take a nymph but, more often than not, the nymph must be placed very accurately to get a reaction. Surface and unseen underwater currents can both contrive to sweep your nymph past a fish and out of sight or range.

In such clear water – often referred to as gin clear – the dark shape of a trout stands out against the clean, stony river bed

Realizing the existence of and overcoming such obstacles is all part of the challenge of upstream nymphing.

Good presentation and accurate casting include casting far enough upstream of a fish so that your nymph has time to sink to the same depth as the fish, and that it will be close enough for the fish to see it. When you cast most nymphs (unless they are very light) they will hit the water with a little splash which shows you where they landed. Knowing where it is makes it much easier to follow its progress downstream.

Only cast as close to a fish as you think you need to, and do try to keep the end of the line behind the fish. Short, accurate casts are best, but not at the expense of getting too close to the fish and frightening it. Sometimes a fish will not see your nymph when you cast to one side of it, but will see it if you cast to the other side. You may at some time find that you have been casting to a fish blind in one eye: a cast to the other side may get the right reaction. There are some fish that, whatever you do and however accurately you cast, cannot be seduced into taking your nymph because they are not hungry or not feeding at that particular time. If you think that is the case, move on to another one.

Detecting the take

One of the most difficult aspects of nymph fishing is knowing when a fish has taken your nymph – detecting a take. A trout can take a nymph with great delicacy and expel it from its mouth with equal expediency. There will be times when you experience a heart-stopping moment when the downstream drift of your leader is checked and it 'draws' under. Instantly you raise your rod to set your hook, unsure whether it is a fish, or your nymph has snagged weed. Almost before you have time to think, a brown trout explodes into action and you know, this time, it was a fish and not weed.

When you are fishing for trout that are feeding on nymphs and you can see them, then detecting the take is relatively easy. You may see the fish move towards your fly, followed by a flash of white as the fish opens its mouth and takes your

Although you may not actually need a wide range of artificial nymphs, it can be helpful to have plenty to choose from

You can sometimes see a fish turn and take your nymph and that may be why they are hooked in the front of their mouths rather than in the scissors. This fish has been hooked right in the scissors

nymph. If you see this, raise your rod tip firmly (but not too aggressively) to set the hook. But you must concentrate and watch the fish all the time, and note where your leader cuts through the surface. This is known as the dipping point. The real challenge of detecting a take is when you are fishing a piece of water in hope, or an unexpected fish seizes your nymph. If you cannot see the fish and the end of your leader stops, is drawn under water, or moves in some other way, again tighten straight away. If it is a fish then it should be hooked firmly in the scissors. Sometimes you will be fooled into tightening into the bottom, or a lump of weed will fly past your ear, but there will be happy times when you think that you have hooked the bottom but then the bottom moves suddenly and you realize that it is a fish. Takes can be very quick and subtle, so you may not always feel anything.

Although the ideal is to cast to a fish (or to fish in the plural) that you can see, or to one that has

shown you where it is by a sub-surface rise, you will not always be able to see the fish.

When wading for example, your range of vision is quite limited as your eyes are closer to the water compared to standing on the bank, and so you do need to be able to detect takes when you can't see fish. Something that can happen is that an unseen fish will turn and follow your nymph downstream. Just as you raise your rod to cast again the fish will lunge at your fly because it thinks it is about to lose a tasty morsel. When this happens it can be impossible to stop yourself making another cast, even if you can see the fish. You end up pulling the nymph away from it. Another thing that can happen – and can be a reason for seemingly failing to hook a fish – is that you cast to a fish, your fly passes the spot where you think the fish is lying and your leader checks. When you tighten there is nothing there. What may have happened is that the fish turned, followed your nymph downstream and took it

facing downstream. As you tightened your line you simply pulled the fly out of its mouth.

When 'fishing the water', or casting to fish which are not showing signs of feeding on nymphs, you need to be alert all the time for anything that suggests a fish has seized your offering. You may actually feel a good firm take from a fish that then moves off with your nymph in its mouth, or the take may just be firm enough to check the downstream passage of your leader, or pull it to one side. There will be times when the take is so gentle that you miss it, or something tells you to set the hook. With practice, concentration and experience, detecting takes will become a sixth sense: you sense or 'feel' that you have a fish on, even if you cannot always see it.

INDICATORS AS AN AID TO CONCENTRATION AND DETECTION

For many newcomers to nymph fishing, detecting a take can seem to be impossible however hard you think you are concentrating on your leader. It's too easy to let your mind wander and your concentration dip and you realize – a fraction of a second too late – that you have just missed a fish. All the time that your artificial nymph is in the river you must concentrate on it – or where you think it is if you can't see it – and on your leader where it cuts through the surface of the water. Fortunately there is a very good way to give yourself something to concentrate on that has the added benefit of amplifying tiny movements in your leader and subtle takes. And that is by using an indicator.

There are many different types of indicator available in a range of colours; some types and colours are better in one set of conditions than another. There are some indicators that are so large that to use one is almost akin to float fishing and it is the use of these indicators that has given the idea of fishing with an indicator a bad name. Fortunately there are indicators that

It is much easier to catch a fish on a nymph if you can actually see the fish in the water

127

do just that – indicate – without having any significant effect on how deep you fish and the way your nymph fishes in the water, the most acceptable indicators were described in Chapter 2. Strike putty is discreet and works well on slow or flat water, but is not the most durable. A few over-vigorous casts may result in it falling from your leader. Alternatively, a short length of indicator yarn can be tied around a knot in your leader (to hold it in place) or tied-in when you add a tippet to the end of the leader. The piece of yarn is then trimmed to length. It is best to leave it a little on the long side as it can then be shortened if required. A yarn indicator is very good when the wind is ruffling water.

As suggested earlier, a short length – 1 in (2.5 cm) or so – of Kahuna LT indicator tube can be built in to your leader and left there permanently. (There are also times when dry-fly fishing that a subtle indicator can be a big help.)

Most of the time the best place to position your indicator is at the bottom end of your leader, or at the top end of the tippet, as you do not want the indicator to stop your nymph from fishing at the required depth.

As well as using an indicator, you must make sure that your leader is well greased, but only up to the tippet. You want it to float as well as possible so that you can see it. If you have a tub of paste-type floatant, hold your leader against the contents with a finger or thumb and draw as much of the leader as you want to grease through it.

You will need to re-grease the leader at intervals throughout a day's fishing. The tippet must not be greased if you are fishing deep water, when you want your nymph to sink as deep as possible, but if you are trying to fish your nymph just under the surface, then you should grease your tippet to within 3 or 4 in (7.5–10 cm) of the end to stop it sinking and make sure that it is close to the surface.

A yarn indicator works best when the water surface is ruffled by a breeze as it will stand up well. One disadvantage is that the yarn looks like a fly and fish will rise to it

An indicator made with a short length of Kahuna LT tube is very low profile

Greasing your leader regularly throughout the day will help to keep it afloat. A high-floating leader signals sub-surface takes very well

Nymph fishermen and women can manage with fewer artificials than the dry fly angler. Top row from left: A gold bead-head gold-ribbed hare's ear and two sizes of gold-ribbed hare's ear nymphs. Bottom row: A copper bead-head, an original Sawyer pheasant tail nymph and a copper bead-head gold-ribbed hare's ear

Basic technique

When fishing on a river where the rule of fishing nymphs upstream only is enforced rigorously, when your nymph is level with where you are standing, that is the end of that cast and you must lift your fly from the water and cast upstream again. If you do not, you may be accused of fishing downstream!

Identifying what fish are feeding on can be tricky, or even impossible, unless flies are hatching, but you won't go far wrong if you start off with a gold-ribbed hare's ear nymph or pheasant tail nymph.

If, after a number of good presentations, the only reaction you are getting is a fish turning to inspect your nymph before leaving it well alone, it is time to change it, either for one of a different size, or another pattern. The frequent inspection is telling you that your artificial is not a good match for what the fish is feeding on.

When you have spotted a (feeding) fish in an approachable lie the objective is to cast your nymph up and across the stream and to allow it to follow a dead drift, at the same speed as the current, back down towards the fish. You should always endeavour to get into a position whereby you can cast up and across at an angle to keep your line and leader away from the fish. Casting straight upstream so that your line lands over or alongside a fish is an easy way to scare it, particu-larly on a sunny day in low water conditions. But with a fish lying under your own bank, unless you can wade into a better position or mount an attack from the opposite bank, there may be no other way than to cast straight upstream. Is there another fish to cast to in a better position? Careful observation may alert you to another fish.

You must retrieve your line as your nymph floats back towards you, something which happens surprisingly quickly in fast-flowing rivers. Make sure that you have the index finger of your rod hand holding the line against the rod handle, while you pull the line, with your line hand, away from the rod and hold it in your hand, in a loose coil. Now trap the line with your rod hand while you move your line hand back to the rod to take hold of the line again so that you can retrieve another coil of line. If you made only a short cast a couple of good retrieves may be all that is needed before making your next cast. A longer cast will require more retrieves. However much line you need to retrieve you must always leave enough line beyond the tip of your rod so that you can cast again. If you retrieve all the line and part of your leader through the top ring of your rod, it will be impossible to make another cast without pulling or shaking some line out beyond the top ring.

As you get near the end of the drift of a nymph, it will help if you raise the tip of your rod

and lift-off straight into your next cast. Doing this will keep you in touch with your nymph and you can speed up your retrieve slightly to get your line moving on the water so that you can make your next cast. The bigger the coils of line that you make as you retrieve, the easier and quicker it is to cast again. You must always keep in touch with your nymph by eliminating unwanted slack in your line because the fish to which you made your cast, or another one, may take your nymph at any time. If you have too much slack line between you and the fish, you may not be able to tighten the line quickly enough to set the hook. It is also important not to retrieve your line so hard or fast that you pull your nymph downstream faster than the current. This will make the nymph's behaviour look very unnatural to a fish. Most nymphs are not Olympic-standard swimmers, able to swim faster than or against the current.

When you lift off and cast again will depend on whether or not your nymph may be seen by other fish but, to ensure that you are always fishing upstream (and not downstream) you must lift off when your nymph is still in front of you. There are occasions when you will only want a short drift and your line may be at an angle of forty-five degrees across the river, while on other occasions you will want to fish out the cast to the bitter end by raising your rod so that only the leader is on the water. Particularly when wading it can be very effective to fish out the cast by raising the rod and then using a roll pick-up followed by one false cast to extend your line further and then completing your cast. The roll pick-up helps load the rod when you have only a short length of line beyond the top ring.

HOW DEEP TO FISH?

It is very important to fish your nymph at the same depth as the fish that you hope to catch. A fish may be happy to move to one side or the other to take a natural nymph – or your artificial

Gold-ribbed hare's ear nymphs are some of the most popular anywhere in the world and can be bought or tied in a range of colours

131

One way to make nymphs sink is to use artificials with metal bead heads. Beads are available in different colours with the most popular being gold, copper and black. Goldheads, as they are known, can be too flashy on sunny days while a copper bead is more muted and is a better choice

– as it passes by, but it will only be an aggressive feeder that will make the effort to rise up in the water to take a nymph that would otherwise pass over its head.

Fish your nymph at the wrong depth and it will be ignored by most fish. This is true of all depths of water, from shallow, skinny water to the slower deep pools and runs. The depth at which a nymph is fished is achieved and controlled by the weight (or lack of) of the artificial, the length of tippet and whether or not part of the leader is greased to make it float. Most artificial nymphs are tied with some added weight to ensure that they sink. The one exception is the pheasant tail nymph, which is tied with copper wire which acts as both tying thread and weight.

Pheasant tail nymphs catch fish feeding on nymphs wherever there are trout to catch

Don't forget to check your nymph every now and then to make sure that it isn't strung-up with weed

Shrimps and caddis larvae live on the bottom of rivers and streams, as do most nymphs until they are ready to head to the surface to hatch, and so your artificial needs to fish near the bottom too. To make sure that a 'hairy' nymph, such as a gold-ribbed hare's ear, sinks straight away, rub some spit into it. If you can see or suspect that your nymph has not sunk properly, a little pull on your fly line should help it to sink. Although it is annoying to keep catching weed it does tell you that your fly is getting down to the bottom of the stream. When this happens you must check your nymph regularly to make sure it is free from weed.

If you can see your nymph and it looks to be getting too close to the bottom, a little lift with your rod tip will make it rise up in the water and keep clear of weed. This is very similar to what is known as an induced take. This is a method of animating your nymph as it approaches a fish.

What you do is raise your rod tip so that your nymph rises up in the water, fooling a fish into thinking that your nymph is going to be swept up and away before it can eat it.

Fish that are 'bulging' and taking nymphs that are hatching, or about to hatch, will be interested in artificials that are fished at the same depth as they are feeding, typically just under or in the surface film. To achieve this, use an artificial that has less weight, or grease the tippet nearly up to the nymph, or use a combination of these methods. This is one time when the use of an unleaded nymph may be called for.

NYMPH AND DRY FLY COMBINATION

Fishing a nymph below a dry fly – a technique developed in New Zealand – can be very effective on days when you are not sure whether to fish a nymph or a dry, or when some fish are feeding on nymphs and others on dries. This method

Lightly weighted nymphs are needed when fish are feeding high in the water rather than close to the bottom

Fishing with a trailer nymph, sometimes known as fishing the duo, can be described as fishing with an active indicator as the dry fly – the indicator – has a hook and will catch fish. Fish will rise to an indicator and, if there is no hook, you will not catch them. This is one of the disadvantages of fishing with an indicator

involves fishing with a dry fly tied to the end of your tippet and a nymph tied to the bend of the hook on a short length – perhaps 18 in (45 cm) – of tippet material. Use the tucked half blood knot to tie the tippet to the hook bend. You should use a bushy dry fly that will not be sunk by the weight of the nymph, particularly in fast or rough water, and although its primary purpose is to act as an indicator, it will catch fish. You can change the sizes of fly and the length of the dropper to suit conditions and the depth at which you need to fish the nymph. Use a longer dropper for deeper water and a shorter one to fish closer to the surface.

WHICH FISH TO TARGET FIRST

If you can see fish in the water but they do not seem to be feeding, how do you decide which fish to cast to? When there is a choice, go for the one that is highest in the water, and therefore nearest the surface. Fish that are high in the water – 'on the fin' – are more likely to be feeding

or at least showing some interest in food. In contrast, fish that are lying very close to the bottom, hardly moving, can be caught but they often need waking up. Next, select the fish that is nearest to you. If there are two or three fish relatively close together and you can hook the one nearest to you, with care and firm control you may be able to keep it away from the other fish and stop it frightening them. But if you hook the one in the middle or furthest away, playing it and getting into a position where you can land it will result in frightening the other fish. When they dash to safety they will probably frighten many other fish too.

At first a certain amount of trial and error will be needed in trying to gauge where to pitch your nymph. Factors to be taken into account are the weight and speed of sink of your artificial, the speed of the current and the depth to which your fly must sink. If you have a fish close to the surface of a medium-paced river, a lightly weighted nymph, such as a pheasant tail nymph, can be

Frank Sawyer's pheasant tail nymph is one of the most dependable nymphs when you want to use an artificial that will not sink too quickly

cast to land closer to the fish as compared to a similar fish in a fast river.

In general, you will have to cast smaller, lighter nymphs further upstream to give them time to sink to the required depth, particularly when they need to sink quite deep. It may not always be possible to do this, so a fish that wants your nymph will have to move to take it and in so doing it may give away its position if you could not see it clearly, or at all.

Two things can upset this measured approach. The first is that the fish takes your nymph the moment that it hits the water. Although this may not happen frequently it happens often enough for you to need to be sure you know what to do. The way to deal with an instant rise is to be always ready to set the hook when you have finished your presentation cast: this means having your line under control all the time. The second thing that can happen is that a fish will make an attempt at your nymph as it disappears past it – or doesn't see it until it is nearly out of sight – and

pursues it downstream. Quite often this will happen as you are just about to raise your rod and lift your line off the water to make another cast. Although you may spot the fish and manage to stop yourself snatching the fly from the fish's jaws, if the fish manages to grab your fly your rod may be too far back to be able to set the hook properly. All that you can do to try to prevent this is to be extremely alert to everything that is happening in the water and hope that you can see a pursuing fish before it is too late.

You must remember to check your hook for bits of weed that it may have picked up, and after you have hooked the bottom. Do make sure that the hook still has a point as it is possible for hooks to break or get broken, for example when fishing rivers where there are rocks and stones. A hook can also get broken if your back cast hits a stone or something hard on the bank behind you. It can be difficult enough to get a fish to take your offering so you do not want to lose it because you had no point on your hook!

CHAPTER NINE

Fishing on stillwaters

For many anglers the most accessible fly fishing will be a stillwater, either a natural or semi-natural lake, a lake created for fishing or a flooded gravel pit. The most interesting and rewarding way to fish these stillwaters is by adopting an imitative approach.

Stillwaters are accessible to most fly fishing beginners and improvers because they are plentiful; many are near large centres of population and they are, in the main, day-ticket waters so access is easy and usually not too expensive. That means you do not have to be a member of a club (although some stillwaters have clubs for members only) and you can either book a ticket in advance or turn up and buy one on the day that you want to fish. Stillwaters and lakes range in size from small ponds perhaps the size of a football pitch to flooded former gravel workings covering a significant area. Although they are fished from the banks most of the time, some of the bigger stillwaters may have boats that anglers can use. Some fisheries have only one lake while others will have a number to offer. The majority are stocked with rainbow trout, but in some you will find brown trout as well, hybrids of the two, and even char.

There are many different ways and techniques you can use to fish stillwaters but imitative methods will nearly always produce results, as well as being the most rewarding and enjoyable.

Most stillwater fisheries are stocked with rainbow trout. They thrive well in clean water where there is plenty of food

As a stillwater angler you need to think about your approach, to be methodical and not to simply cast out and retrieve time after time. For those who take a little time to look around and observe what is, or is not happening, there will nearly always be clues as to where the fish are, or where they might be expected to be, and what they might be feeding on. Fishing without thinking and therefore not catching any fish will lead only to frustration and then anger. Don't rush to the water without thinking, as you may frighten any fish that are feeding close to the bank. When you are on the bank and before you make your first cast, you should always look into the water by where you are standing to see what nymphs, larvae, other forms of fly life and small fish are in evidence before deciding which fly or flies to use. Some days there will be plenty of life to see; on others, not very much at all. At the same time take a close look at the edge of the water by the bank, where you may see discarded caddis cases, nymphal shucks and even stillborn

flies and dead spent flies. And don't forget to have a good look around during the course of the day, keeping an eye open for anything that has changed, or new arrivals. On windy days you may find various terrestrials are being blown onto the water.

The water in small stillwaters is affected much more than that in rivers by changes in temperature and the weather in general. The temperature will affect how near the surface or how deep the fish are likely to be feeding. Early in the season when the water is cold, wind-generated currents tend to draw warmer water to the surface. When the water is very cold, fish will try to find warmer areas but, conversely, if the water starts to get too warm (in high summer) fish will seek out cooler water and areas where there is more oxygen. If the water temperature rises too high, some stillwaters will close to fishing because catching fish in very warm water simply increases the stress on them to unacceptable levels. A few days of cooler weather or some heavy rain will often be enough

Small stillwaters usually provide fairly accessible fly fishing for many thousands of anglers. It is very easy to waste a lot of time moving from place to place on a stillwater because you have seen, or heard, a fish rise on the other side of the lake. Sometimes moving will bring success but it can be just as effective to stay put and wait for cruising fish to find your fly or flies

to lower the temperature so that angling can start again.

If it is impossible to see the bottom and therefore you are not sure of the depth of water, it is worth remembering that deeper water is usually darker in colour: the deeper the water the darker the colour. Once the weeds have started to grow it will be easier to find the shallower areas as most weeds do not grow in very deep water.

Standing on the banks of a stillwater it is just as important (most particularly when the water is clear) as it is on the riverbank to check where the sun is and where your shadow is falling. You may also need to take advantage of any bankside cover to conceal yourself or break up your outline, particularly when the water is clear and shallow. The position and height of the sun will also influence where you should be fishing. Shady areas are best fished during the day, and areas fully exposed to the sun in the early mornings or evenings. Fish are affected by the sun and, in clear water on bright sunny days, they will probably be

found deeper in the water, where the effect of the sun's rays is less as compared to nearer the surface – although they will be found close to the surface if there is plenty of food available.

Small man-made lakes and flooded gravel pits tend to be somewhat lacking in underwater features compared to reservoirs which have been made by, for example, damming and flooding a valley, where there will be signs of old hedges, ditches and even streams and perhaps the odd building. Some of these features can be identified by studying an old map of the area and by walking the shore, particularly at times of very low water. But even in small stillwaters the water has to come from somewhere, so look for an inlet, or outlet, or springs bubbling up from the lake bed, as these are all features that will be attractive both to food forms and the trout themselves.

When fishing a stillwater on a windy day you want to stand on the leeward shore so that you are casting into the wind. Why make life hard for yourself by casting into the wind? The answer is

Most stillwaters will have a water inlet which will bring food items into the water as well as fresh oxygen-rich water

Fishing when there is a nice ripple on the surface, as here, is easier than fishing in a flat calm

very simple: you will be fishing where the fish are, and nothing is more important if you want to catch fish. Food items and the whole body of water will be blown by the wind so the fish line up along the lee shore, facing into the wind, eating every nymph or fly that is blown towards them. Also, they will often cruise upwind before turning to swim back to where they started and repeating the whole procedure. By contrast, fishing on the windward shore, with your back to the wind, you are more than likely to be casting to water where there are no, or only a few, fish. Some books get windward and leeward muddled up. Anyone with a knowledge of sailing will know that the old tea clippers such as the *Cutty Sark* were always terrified of being driven onto a lee shore – rounding Cape Horn for example – as their ability to sail to windward and escape the clutches of the lee shore was quite limited. Square-rigged sailing ships had even greater problems sailing to windward.

Casting into strong winds will call for high line speed – the double haul will help achieve this – and tight, aerodynamic loops which you can punch into the wind. Aiming your presentation cast low will also help by getting it below the wind as quickly as possible. On windy days when there is likely to be a good ripple – if not something of a chop on the water – a splashy presentation isn't going to frighten fish in the same way that it would in very calm conditions.

Strong winds can stir up the bottom of a lake and the muddy water is not going to be appreciated by the fish, whose range of vision will be very limited, although bottom-living creatures may be swept from their homes and into circulation. If you think that the wind is too strong to cast into, it may be possible to change position to where you can cast less directly into or across the wind, and still work your flies to where the fish are feeding. The right-hand caster wants to find a place where the wind is blowing from left to right – this will ensure that the line and fly is blown away from the angler's head and face – and the

left-hander wants a wind blowing from right to left for the same reason. On days that are not very windy it is less important where you decide to fish.

One exception to fishing into the wind is if there are trees and bushes around the shore or bank as these may hold caterpillars, terrestrials and other forms of food that will be blown onto the water by a strong wind, so you can afford to fish with the wind on your back. As well as expecting this to happen you must keep looking to see what is being blown onto the water.

In the same way that, when fishing a river, you should fish your way into the stretch you intend to wade, when fishing a stillwater you should start by fishing the water by your feet before contemplating a cast to the other side of the lake. The fish at the far side of a given piece of water are no different from those close to your feet, which the angler opposite you is trying to catch when his or her fly lands with a splash near you. Trying to cast to the far side of a piece of water every time is not only hard work but also unnecessary, as there will probably be fish within sensible casting distance.

Be on your guard for fish that follow your fly right into the bank and make a grab for it as you are about to lift-off and cast again. In some ways this could be described as the reverse of catching fish on the drop (this is when a fish takes your fly as it sinks through the water) and it's not just fish in rivers that do this. As mentioned earlier, the problem when this happens is that it can be very difficult to stop your back cast so that you don't simply yank the fly out of the fish's reach.

Fishing your fly, or flies, at the right depth is likely to be very much more effective than an ability to cast a full line every time. Depth is much more important than distance. Fish feed on living organisms that can rise and fall in the water column as they make their way to the surface to hatch. This may happen for some time and then these same insects change behaviour and perhaps stay at a greater depth and the fish follow them into deeper water. If you find that

It isn't always necessary to make long casts as some fish will feed close to the bank

*Playing a good fish on a
sunny late autumn day*

under water or away from you, or suddenly realize that you can feel something on the end of your line. When this happens, raise your rod and set the hook and all being well you will have a fish on your line.

Some words of caution: A stillwater angler's movements along the bank, or when he or she is going to cast again, are much less predictable than those of a river angler. This makes it important to be very aware of what other anglers are doing. Stillwater anglers do not have the same imperative to keep moving slowly upstream in the way that river anglers do. On a stillwater you might decide on a change of place or even go back to your car for a drink. If you do make a move and pass close by another angler, alert him or her to your presence, or make sure that you are well out of range of a back cast. By the same token, if you are fishing and about to lift-off and cast again, do check that there is not someone walking behind you who might get hit with your fly.

On a quiet, still day some people will be quite surprised to discover just how well sound travels over water – so be careful what you say if you have a loud voice!

Stillwater tackle

Although it is quite possible – and enjoyable – to fish many small stillwaters and lakes with standard river tackle, the more determined and committed stillwater angler will want to buy a longer rod that is capable of casting longer distances. A 9½ ft (2.9 m) or even a 10 ft (3 m) rod for a #6 or #7 line will fit the bill.

A larger size of reel will be necessary for these heavier weights of line as well as allowing more backing to be fitted. You may also want to consider buying an intermediate or slow-sinking line as well as a floating line. What are known as cassette reels are a very practical response to the problem of carrying a range of different lines. A cassette reel has a basic metal frame and is usually sold with two or sometimes three lightweight plastic spools, or cassettes, which hold the fly line and can be interchanged quickly and easily. These cassettes are much cheaper than spare spools for non-cassette reels.

you are not getting any pulls on your line or actually hooking fish, it may be time to try fishing at a different depth. The reverse can happen when fish move from feeding well down to close to the surface, perhaps following hatching buzzers as they rise to the surface. You need to be aware of what is happening and be prepared to follow the fish.

The stillwater angler needs to be patient, to concentrate hard and, above all, stay alert. The take of a cruising rainbow trout can be very gentle and subtle: you may see your leader drawn

Intermediate lines are very useful as they will not create a wake in the surface when retrieved on calm days and, if there is enough breeze to ruffle the surface, the intermediate line will sink below any moving water and so will not be pushed by the wind. This means that you can retrieve your line in a straight line (unlike a floating line which will tend to be blown in a big arc by the wind), and also at a more constant depth. Sink-tip and sinking lines are used to fish greater depths than can be reached using a floating line and a sinking leader. Fast sinkers will

A longer rod, for a heavier weight of fly line, will help you to cast further and so enable you to get your fly to fish well out from the bank

Surface breezes will often move your fly line faster than you want as well as blow a dry fly across the surface

143

If you are fishing with a long leader and two or more flies, a long-handled landing net will be the only way to reach a fish so that you can net it

Casting and fishing with a very long leader is going to be beyond the scope of the newly initiated. Instead of trying to fish straight away with a very long leader, start with one of about 10 ft (3m) and gradually extend it as you gain experience and confidence. An extended river leader will be satisfactory for fishing a single (sunk) fly or dry-fly fishing, but when fishing with a team of flies you can use a level, untapered leader quite satisfactorily as the weight of the flies will ensure that the leader (as long as it is of an adequate *thickness* not strength) turns over properly. This will happen only if you have the heaviest fly on the point (the business end of the leader) and the lightest fly, or flies, on the dropper(s). The minimum breaking strain for your tippet should not be less than 5 lb (2.27 kg).

For fishing with more than one fly, the dropper, or droppers, want to be about 5 ft (1.5 m) apart and each dropper needs to be about 8 or 9 in (20 or 23 cm) in length. A dropper of this length keeps the fly away from the leader and is also long enough to allow a number of changes of fly. If you make a dropper too short, after a change or two of fly it will be too short to use again and you will have to make up a new leader, most probably in the middle of the best hatch of the day. But do not try to fish with over-long droppers as they are more likely to wrap themselves round the leader. You can use the surgeon's knot to make your droppers by leaving long tag ends and cutting the end pointing up towards the fly line: the end pointing down is used as the dropper.

You may wonder how you will manage to land a fish when using a very long leader. If you try to fish with a *very* long leader it will be all but impossible, but if you fish with a three-fly leader with each fly 5 ft (1.5 m) apart, that means that the point fly will be about 10 ft (3 m) from the top of your rod when you have wound-in the line and leader to the first dropper. If you catch a fish on the point fly, assuming that you have a landing net with a long handle, with your rod arm fully extended up and behind you, you will just about be able to reach it with your net, If you can't, you will have to beach your fish by walking backwards, pulling the fish into the bank as you go.

reach greater depths more quickly as well as allowing a small, light fly to be fished at depth.

The other big difference between river and stillwater fly fishing is the design of leader. For many years now stillwater anglers have been using very long leaders, sometimes up to 30 ft (9.1 m) in length, and regularly between 18 and 20 ft (5.5 and 6.1 m), so roughly twice as long as a river angler would use. When using a long leader, make sure that the connection between fly line and leader is as smooth as possible so that it will pass through the rod rings when landing a fish.

The importance of the retrieve

Along with fishing in the right place – i.e. where there are, or you hope there will be, feeding fish – and at the right depth, the way that you retrieve your fly or flies is a crucial aspect of stillwater fly fishing. Retrieves include the classic and very versatile figure-of-eight and the static retrieve through to fast retrieves. Each one has its uses and optimum conditions. The idea of the static retrieve is to cast out, remove any slack from the line and then do nothing more than watch and wait for a take, all the time making sure that you keep in touch with your fly, or flies, but without moving them. Holding the line between your thumb and forefinger will help you to feel for any slight movement at the end of the line. When fishing on moving water as in a river or stream, most of the retrieve is concerned with eliminating slack from the line and keeping in contact with your fly so that, should a fish rise and take your fly, you can set the hook. On stillwaters, as well as keeping in contact with your fly, you need to be able to use a range of retrieves to impart different movements or motion, or indeed none at all.

As you gain experience you will soon be able to match the speed and style of your retrieve to suit the prevailing conditions including the weather, what type of flies you are fishing and the depth at which you are fishing.

When fishing nymphs or buzzers you need to know how deep they are in the water and to be able to keep fishing at that depth. The way to do this is to count down after you make a cast so that you can fish again at the same depth. You make a cast, count to say ten and then start your retrieve. If you feel a touch or catch a fish, the next time that you cast and count to ten, your fly should be in the same zone. Vary the depth you fish until you catch a fish and then repeat the same countdown so your fly is at the same depth again. As I read in an American magazine: 'Trout may be spread throughout the water column, but there is likely a depth where the fish can find the best groceries.' Although

Concentration and holding your fly line all the time so that you can feel gentle takes will help you to catch fish. When fishing a nymph, or team of nymphs, straighten your line but don't tighten it, and allow the fly or flies to sink to the required depth. Depending on the depth of water you are fishing, it may take longer than you think for the fly on the end of your leader to reach that depth

145

Here the wind is blowing from right to left and has swept the line round in a big curve. When this happens it can make detecting takes difficult and hinder quick hook sets. Both factors will result in fewer fish being hooked

you may have found the optimum depth, don't be surprised if it alters during the course of the day, particularly if the weather is unstable and changing.

One disadvantage of fishing a sunk fly on a floating line is the difficulty of retrieving your fly at the same depth, unless you retrieve it very slowly and gently. As the speed of retrieve increases there will be a natural tendency for your fly to rise up the water column so leaving the crucial depth at which the fish are feeding. Sometimes this effect can be reduced by fishing a heavier fly which will rise in the water more slowly; alternatively using an intermediate or sink-tip line as the sunk or part-sunk line will create less lift.

The figure-of-eight retrieve is made with your line hand by retrieving line with your first finger and thumb and holding that line in the palm of your hand while you move your finger and thumb up the line and retrieve another few inches of line, which you gather into the palm of your hand with your free fingers. You will find that the line looks

like a figure-of-eight in your hand, hence the name of this retrieve. Always make sure that you hold the line against the rod handle with the forefinger of your rod hand so that you can trap the line to set the hook. With practice you can retrieve line in a smooth, continuous motion from the very slowest speed to a fly's equivalent of a submarine or speedboat.

Slow, smooth retrieves should be your aim most of the time, but there will be times when a more stop-start retrieve is very effective. Such a retrieve will allow your fly to sink a little between pulls. Short pulls of 1 in (25 mm) or so of line can be made to represent a nymph darting about, while a slightly longer pull of a foot or so (30 cm) could be another nymph trying to swim to the surface to hatch. The pause represents the nymph dropping back to have a rest before making another effort to reach the surface.

The effect of a steady crosswind on your line will be that of a very desirable slow, continuous retrieve, as long as you remove any slack in the line so gently that it doesn't affect the fly. On

windy days you may find that a floating line is being blown too quickly by the wind. You can counteract this to some extent by mending your line into the wind to reduce some, or all, of the downwind curve.

Bloodworms and buzzers should be fished either with the slowest possible retrieve or no retrieve at all – static. Takes will often be almost imperceptible and as a consequence you will miss many fish simply because you were not aware that your fly had been taken. Fish will take a buzzer as it sinks just after you have cast, so you need to be prepared for this by managing your line properly. You can't afford to drop your line and then have to look down while you pick it up and get organized, as you will most likely miss hooking a fish that takes your fly on the drop. (Midges are ubiquitous on stillwaters and although there are so many different members of the Chironomidae family, they are so similar in shape that it is only necessary to carry a range of imitations in different sizes and colours.)

Assuming that you are using suitable tackle, and are fishing in the right place with the most suitable choice of fly or flies, you are still not going to catch fish unless you concentrate on the end of your line and the leader, as it will very often be the subtle movement that tells you that you have a fish on. If your fly is near the surface, you may see a slight boil as a fish rises to take it, but although some will be, not all takes are smash takes that nearly wrench the rod out of your hand. Coupled with the concentration of watching for the slightest of movement is the need for a delicate touch on the line with the thumb and first finger of your rod hand, feeling for anything happening underwater. It's the subtle, delicate takes as a fish 'mouths' your fly that are all too easy to miss, and for which you must be alert. If you raise your rod to set the hook every time you have the slightest suspicion that you might have hooked a fish, you will probably hook and land fish more often than finding there is nothing on the end of your line except a fly.

Fish in stillwaters can feed consistently for a while and then stop, often for no apparent reason. Then, after a while, they will start feeding again

147

Essential stillwater flies. Top row, from left: yellow Montana nymph, gold bead-head damsel nymph, red Shipman's buzzer, black Shipman's buzzer. Middle row: orange Montana nymph, gold-ribbed hare's ear nymph, brown Shipman's buzzer, Adams dry fly. Bottom row: Red diawl bach nymph, gold bead-head gold-ribbed hare's ear nymph, pheasant tail nymph, epoxy black buzzer, epoxy red buzzer

Stillwater techniques

There are two main imitative ways to fish stillwaters: with nymphs and buzzer patterns close to or below the surface and dry flies on the top of the water. In the spring and early summer fishing with a nymph, or team of nymphs (that is one nymph on the end of your leader and another one or two on droppers) or buzzer pupae, fished deep and very slowly is likely to be the most effective way of catching trout. The time to think about fishing with a dry fly is exactly the same as on a river: when you can see flies hatching and floating on the water and fish are rising and feeding on them.

FISHING NYMPHS AND BUZZERS

When fishing a team of buzzers make sure that all your flies – on the point and droppers – are well-spaced apart as this allows you to search for fish at a range of depths, and one fly moving in an unnatural manner may not be seen by a fish higher or lower in the water. Two flies close together behaving oddly may be more obvious. Finding the right depth is very important. Once you have found the optimum depth, use the countdown method mentioned earlier so that you can continue to fish at roughly the same depth. When fishing buzzers static it can be a

On a clear bank it is easy to make long casts. But if there are trees behind you, casting will be more of a challenge

A full-finned, over-wintered brown trout. It is very important to find the depth at which fish are feeding and then to keep fishing at that depth. But be prepared to change depth if you stop getting any interest from the fish

good idea to give your line a slow pull of about 3 ft (1m) to lift your flies in the water column and then stop so that they will fall back slowly, like a natural rising and falling on its way to the surface. Also it relieves the monotony of simply standing waiting to feel a fish take your fly. A fish might respond to a rising buzzer or one falling after you have taken a pull.

Another popular way to fish buzzers is to use what is known as a washing line. You do this by replacing the heavy buzzer on the end, or point, of your leader with a floating fly. The buzzer, or buzzers, on the dropper(s) will then hang down from your leader just under the surface. You can leave your line to drift with any breeze, or use a very slow figure-of-eight retrieve. This technique can be used when fish can be seen high in the water and their backs will be seen sometimes when they feed on rising buzzers.

On days when there is a breeze or wind blowing, try to make the best use of that breeze. Apart from when the wind is blowing on your back, you can cast out, tighten your line and let the wind move your flies, instead of simply retrieving them back to the bank.

You can increase or decrease the speed of your line and flies by casting more, or less, across or into the wind. A drift can be extended by mending the line into the wind. The faster a floating line is moved by the breeze, the higher in

the water the flies will be. If the breeze is too slight to produce enough movement, then you will need to retrieve line slowly to keep the flies fishing at the depth and speed that you want.

As the season develops and air and water temperatures rise, more food forms will be found higher in the water column and just below or on the surface. Fish will follow the food towards the surface and also start to come much closer to the banks, where food items may fall on the water or be blown from bankside vegetation. If, or when, it is possible to find a stretch of bank that is undisturbed, it will be worthwhile fishing *along*, or parallel to the bank, rather than straight out in the lake. Where the water is clear and the light good, it should be possible to identify and stalk individual fish and cast to them selectively as they cruise along. This is a very exciting, skilful and rewarding way to catch often specimen fish. Specialized techniques and flies have been developed to take advantage of specific fish that can be seen and cast to. When stalking fish in clear water you will need to make the best use of any bankside cover so that the fish are less likely or able to see you.

As you are likely to be casting to fish quite close to you, if you fish with a very long leader you will not have enough fly line outside the rod tip to be able to cast accurately, so this is one time when a shorter leader will pay dividends. There will be

A rainbow trout takes a natural fly on the surface. The fish could be seen swimming towards the fly as it floated on the surface. Stillwater fishing is very different from river fishing, one reason being that you are less sure where the fish are and in which direction they are swimming

times when it will be possible to set an ambush for a cruising fish. You can do this by observing quietly the fish's route as it patrols its territory and then casting a nymph or buzzer into its path and allowing it to sink to the bottom. Wait for the fish to return and, as it approaches your offering, slowly lift it towards the surface with the tip of your rod. All being well, the fish will respond with a positive take but, if it does not, let your fly sink again and wait for the fish to continue its patrol and return again. Some fish will respond to a well-placed fly as it sinks in front of them as long as it is cast accurately and allowed to sink to the same depth as the fish.

If you find that you are struggling to interest and catch fish you will waste less valuable fishing time if you change your method of presentation and retrieve rather than keeping changing fly or flies. After a few changes of fly you may even need to replace your tippet or droppers, which wastes even more fishing time.

DRY-FLY FISHING

One advantage of dry-fly fishing is that you can get away with a shorter leader because, when fish are moving about and feeding high in the water, their field of view is much less than when they are deeper down. Also, because you will be fishing your fly either static, or very nearly so, your leader will cause less disturbance than one that is being retrieved all the time. Casting and leaving your fly alone is setting a trap for any fish that swims along and sees it. It may take time, and require placing your fly in a few different places before a fish finds it but, given some patience, a fish will find it eventually.

Make sure when you apply floatant to your fly that you do not get any on the foot or so (30 cm) of tippet nearest your fly. In fact it is a good idea to de-grease this portion of the tippet using a pinch of mud from the bank or a proprietary de-greasing compound or sinkant so that the tippet sinks below the surface where it will be less visible to fish.

One big difference between fishing dry flies on stillwaters compared to rivers is that you are not always sure of the direction in which a fish is swimming when it takes your fly. In a river, nine time out of ten, fish will be facing into the current so when you set the hook you will pull it back into the fish's mouth or the scissors. But in stillwaters, although fish have a tendency to swim into the wind, it is possible that a fish will be pointing at you as it rises and takes your fly. If you try to set the hook too quickly you may simply pull the fly out of its mouth before it has had a chance to turn down. If the water is clear and your fly is not too far away it may be possible to see a fish actually taking your fly.

It can often pay to fish an emerger pattern on a dropper with a dry fly on the point, or another dry on a second dropper. This way you can fish with the emerger held high in the water by the two dry flies, one either side, and hope to attract fish concentrating on emerging flies as well as those feeding on the surface. If you have a dry fly on the point and one dropper, with a nymph on it, that fly will hang motionless just below the surface. By changing the positions of the two flies so that the sinking nymph is on the point and the dry on the dropper, the nymph will sink slowly to a much greater depth. If you then find that the nymph is sinking the dry fly, you can use either a lighter nymph or a more buoyant dry fly, or both.

It is exciting to see a fish rise so close and clearly. In general, trout in stillwaters do not need to rise as aggressively as their cousins in rivers as there is no current to sweep a fly away from them. Even when fish can be seen – and heard – jumping clear of the water, the rise of a rainbow to a dry fly or buzzer can be very subtle, often only a slight boil in the surface

The sun sets over a small stillwater to bring a successful day to a stunning end

CHAPTER TEN

When things go wrong

Unfortunately things do go wrong from time to time. When something does go wrong, the first thing to do is nothing. Stop and assess the problem before doing anything that might make things worse.

Snagging your fly

A very common problem for the new fly angler is that their fly lands on the bank or a piece of vegetation. They either misjudge the distance or a gust of wind blows their cast awry. (And don't forget that casting so that the fly lands on bankside vegetation *on purpose* and then tweaking it free so that it drops on the water can be a very effective tactic – so long as it does tweak free.) For many, the initial reaction to a snagged fly will be to give the rod, or line, a good pull. Sometimes this will work and your fly will come free. More often all you will achieve is driving the point of the hook deeper into whatever is holding it, making it more difficult to recover. But if you pull hard enough you might break the tippet and lose your fly, or if you are really unfortunate, the top section of your rod. So instead of starting to tug and pull straight away, stop and try to find the cause of the problem. If your fly has landed lightly on a blade of grass or piece of vegetation overhanging the water, very often a gentle tug, or tweak, will free it and it may then fall onto the water.

Flies caught more firmly in trees and bushes can often still be rescued with a little patience again, as long as you don't simply pull the hook further into the branch by pulling too hard, too soon. If a straight pull

When your fly gets caught on the bank or snagged on vegetation do resist the temptation to give your rod and line a great yank in the hope of freeing your fly. It will work on occasions but more often you will you will simply drive the hook deeper into whatever it is caught on

When freeing your fly from a tree pull the line gently and do not use your rod as though you are playing a fish. If the fly is not too high in the tree it is often possible to pull the line carefully and get the end of the branch within reach. You can then pull the branch lower and release your fly. Trying to retrieve a fly by pulling hard risks not only overloading the tippet and breaking it, but also damaging your leader which may end up with permanent kinks and coils

won't free it, you may need to slacken your line and manoeuvre your rod so that you can get hold of the line outside the rod tip and pull on the line. If you have snagged something on or near your own bank, all being well you will be able to pull whatever your fly is fastened to close enough for you to reach out and free it. If you do snag your fly on your own bank, for example when lifting-off to cast again, and you have to go upstream to free it, try to make sure that you keep out of sight so as not to frighten any fish.

Sometimes when your fly ends up in a tree the problem can be made worse because the leader is wrapped around the branch as a result of centrifugal force. If this has happened simply pulling won't achieve anything, unless the leader has taken only one or perhaps two turns. It may be possible to pull the branch

When your fly and leader get wrapped around a branch, or a barbed-wire fence, you will have to take time to unwrap them. You won't be able to simply pull the fly free

down low enough to get hold of it so that you can reach up to unwrap the leader and free your fly. You can have the same problem when you catch a barbed wire fence with your back cast, but at least you can get close to the fence and unwrap your fly with a little care.

If you pull too hard on the leader the wrong way and tighten the muddle, when you free your fly you may have to cut off the end of the tippet if it looks like a happy pig's curly tail.

When you are fishing nymphs, particularly heavily weighted ones, or in shallow water, it is quite easy to hook the bottom, a rock or stone, or even a piece of submerged tree branch. Sometimes you may have thought that a fish had taken your fly but it was, in fact, the bottom catching your hook. If this happens, pull off from your reel a number of rod-lengths of line and then make an energetic roll cast upstream. The hope is that as the cast unrolls it will pull your fly upstream and free it from whatever is holding it. It may not work every time but it is always worth a try. When it does work it saves you having to make your way upstream to find and unhook your fly and perhaps frightening a fish or two.

Tangles

One of the downsides of fly fishing is the propensity for things getting in tangles: lines and leaders are the chief culprits. Fly lines and leaders can get knotted and in a tangle, sometimes referred to as a bird's nest, and wrapped round bits of vegetation — rosebay willowherb is one of the worst.

Although protecting rivers and their banks from stock damage with barbed wire fences is a good thing, they are a trap for the unwary angler

Left One of the worst things about fly fishing is how easy it can be to get your leader and line in a real tangle. If you get your tippet or leader or both in a knotted mess, it can be quicker and easier to unravel if you remove your fly first

Patience is needed to undo a major tangle without damaging the line or leader. Knots in your leader need removing as soon as possible as they can weaken it enough to result in it breaking. If there are any knots that are so tight that they cannot be undone, replace the tippet straight away. Sometimes a serious tangle of a leader can be undone quickest by cutting the fly off the end of the tippet. It keeps the hook out of the way and means that you can work the mono free without having to worry about the fly.

Something else that can happen from time to time is your fly line lassoing the end of your rod. To sort things out, place the butt of your rod on the ground and walk up to the tip of the rod. You now need to take hold of the right piece of line and pass it back over the top ring and then make sure that everything is straight again.

Sometimes fly lines seem to have a mind of their own and manage to wrap themselves around the tip of your rod every now and then

Stuck ferrule

Something that you probably will not discover until the end of the day, when you try to take your rod down, is that one of the ferrules has stuck. This can be caused by a tiny bit of grit or dirt jamming the ferrule or, on a very hot day, the male part of the ferrule may have swelled just enough to stick tight. If you think that the cause might be heat, you could try packing ice around the joint – if any is available – but a more practical solution is to put the offending sections of rod in the water in the hope that they will cool enough to come apart. At worse, take the rod home and set about parting the joints there.

When you are trying to part the two sections of a rod, never try to hold either section with anything mechanical such as a pair of pliers or in a vice: both could crush the rod wall. You also need to make sure that you pull the sections in a straight line, without bending them. This is particularly important if two people try to separate a joint. You can get a much better grip on a rod blank if you wear washing-up gloves or use a small piece of sheet rubber such as is sold for opening jar lids. One technique to try when you are on your own is to place the rod behind your knees and grasp the rod on either side. Now, as you pull with both hands, force your knees apart sideways to increase the power that you can apply. If there is someone available to help, stand facing each other and take hold of the opposite sections of the rod and pull them apart by pushing away from you. Holding the sections like this reduces the twisting or bending motion.

Loose ferrule

The opposite of the previous problem is when your rod comes apart while you are fishing. However carefully you assemble your rod there will come a time when it decides to come apart as you are casting. When this happens for the first time it is very disconcerting. Immediate thoughts are that you have broken the rod or

You can sort things out by passing the right piece of line back over the end of your rod

lost a section. But if you look along the length of the fly line you will, all being well, see the wayward section (or sections). If this happens when you are wading it is easy to lean over and pick up the missing section. But when you are fishing from the bank you will have to recover your fly line and the section with it. All being well your fly will engage in a rod guide as you pull on the line and so bring the section with it. When you reassemble your rod make sure that the joints are all given a slight twist to tighten them. It is always a good idea to check the joints during a day's fishing in case one is working loose.

Repairing breathable waders on the inside is less unsightly than doing so on the outside and it also helps to protect the repair

Self-hooking

At some time we will all manage to hook ourselves somewhere: on a hand or even the back of an ear. When this happens, the hook can usually be removed quickly with the right technique. This one is used by commercial long-line fishermen. You need a length of thin string or strong line (your strongest tippet material?) which you loop round the bend of the hook. Press down on the eye of the hook and then make sure that your loop of line is right up at the top of the bend. Still pressing down on the hook eye, give the line a sharp tug away from the eye of the hook. The hook should pop out as long as you have pulled hard enough.

A variation on this method uses a pair of forceps. Again, press down on the eye of the hook and grasp the top of the bend of the hook with the forceps, with your palm up. Twist your wrist sharply and firmly towards the eye of the hook so that your palm finishes facing down-

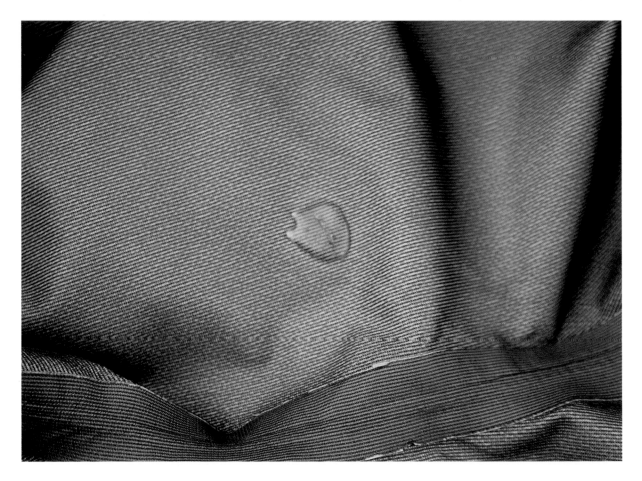

wards. The hook will be out of the flesh. I know from practical experience that this method does work. I was fishing with a friend one summer's evening and as we walked to the river we discussed the best way to carry a fly rod: tip forwards or backwards (see Chapter 6). Just then my friend stumbled and the tip of his rod, complete with a Grey Wulff in the tip ring, made contact with my face. I was well hooked in the cheek! I got him to put the butt of his rod on the ground while I gave him my forceps. I held the eye of the hook while he took hold of the bend and with a deft tweak removed it from my cheek. It didn't hurt – although there was a fair amount of blood – and it has left no mark.

Punctured waders

Even the best and most expensive waders can get punctured. The first sign that your waders have sprung a leak is most likely to be a damp patch on your trousers when you take them off. Breathable waders are susceptible to very fine punctures by thistles, brambles, gorse and anything else that has fine, sharp prickles or spikes, not to forget barbed wire. A tear or hole that is big enough to see can be repaired quite easily, but it is the pin-pricks that are not so easy to find that are more difficult. One way to find them is to turn your waders inside out and then fill each leg in turn with water. This means that you can then make the repair on the inside, which is less unsightly than repairing the outside.

As soon as you see water appearing, mark the spot with a ballpoint pen, then empty the water out and leave the waders to dry. When properly dry you can apply a layer of Aquasure or a similar waterproof repair adhesive to the perforated area.

In an emergency, tears or holes can be patched temporarily with a length of duct or gaffer tape and then repaired more permanently at home. Another very useful product for making quick repairs on the water is Snowbee's Suncure Wader Repair which is a clear, flexible urethane-type material that is cured by UV light, within a few seconds on a sunny day and in up to five minutes in lower UV light conditions.

Falling in

If you have the misfortune to lose your footing and fall in, or fall over or step into an unexpected deep hole in the riverbed when wading and you find your waders full of water, don't panic. If the current is strong, adopt a feet first half-sitting, half-lying position and let yourself go with the current. Having you feet first means that you can see where you are going and can try to steer or paddle yourself into the bank. All being well you will find a place with a low bank where you can crawl out. If you are wearing chest waders and they are full of water, the weight of water will make it impossible to stand up and climb out of the river: you will need to crawl up the bank and then roll over onto your back, raise your legs in the air and drain the water from your waders.

CHAPTER ELEVEN

Looking after your tackle

Most items of your tackle require very little maintenance to keep them working to maximum efficiency. Regular maintenance will keep everything in good condition.

Most fishing tackle is best stored in the dark away from sunlight, in a cupboard or somewhere dry, relatively dust-free and not too cold. Fly lines and tippet material should always be out of direct sunlight. Beware of storing waders in garages or the garden shed where mice might decide to take up residence or make a meal of them.

Rods

At the end of a day's fishing, try to make sure that your rod is dry before you put it in its bag or tube. If you have to put it in the bag still wet, leave it open so that it can dry as quickly as possible. If necessary, take the rod out of its bag when you get back home and dry it with a towel. When it is thoroughly dry, put it in its bag and then in its protective tube. Soap and water and an old toothbrush can be used to clean dirt that has built-up around rod rings or the reel seat. Don't forget to dry the rod thoroughly after washing it.

Like fly lines, cork rod handles pick up an awful lot of grime through the course of a season. But with care and the right method, virtually any cork handle can be made to look like new again. The best way is to use very fine – 400 grit – wet-and-dry abrasive paper which is used by car body-shops when respraying cars. As well as cleaning the handle, sanding gently will remove any ridges or high spots. Wrap some masking

The handle of this well-used rod is in a need of a jolly good clean

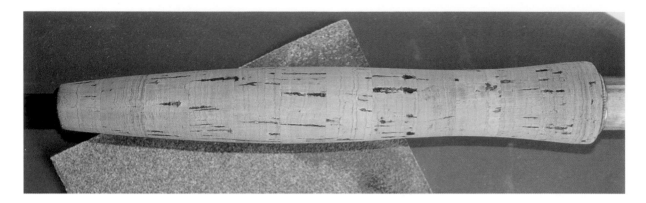

tape around the rod immediately above the handle and around any exposed parts of the reel seat. Take a small piece of wet-and-dry and soak it in warm water and then start to sand the handle parallel to the rod tube, rotating the rod at the same time so that you do not start to flatten the cork. Keep wetting the paper and rubbing gently until the handle is clean. When you are happy with the result, wash the handle in clean water, dry with a towel or cloth and then leave the rod to dry thoroughly before putting it away in its bag.

When you have finished cleaning the handle, if there are any bits of cork missing or a bit of filler has come out, holes and cracks can be filled with cork-coloured wood filler such as Plastic Wood, which can be bought in small tubes or little tins.

Reel care

One of the biggest problems with a reel can be getting sand or grit in the bearings. Although you will see photographs in magazines showing rods and reels in the water, lying on a riverbed, this is one of the easiest ways to guarantee getting sand into the reel.

The more expensive the reel, the more complex the drag system will be, with more parts to be damaged by fine grains of sand. Always try to keep your reel out of the water.

When lubricating a disc drag reel which relies on friction to work, be very careful not to use too much lubricant and make sure that it does not get into the drag mechanism, as it could ruin it.

the dressing. Hang the line in large loops so that it can dry. If the line that you have bought was not supplied with a line dressing, it is easy to buy one from fishing tackle shops.

Fly lines collect kinks which also affect casting performance. Kinks can be removed, or prevented to some degree, by pulling the line off the reel and stretching it at the start of the day. Another thing to do is, again, to pull the line off the reel, drop it in the river and let it hang in the current for a few minutes, before reeling it back onto the reel.

Reviving flies

When the hackles on dry flies get squashed, they can be perked up by holding the fly in a jet of steam from a kettle or saucepan of boiling water. When using a saucepan replace the lid with a piece of cooking foil. Make sure that it is a tight fit all the way around the pan except for a small gap for the steam to escape. Do hold the fly by the bend of the hook with a pair of forceps so that you do not burn your fingers in the steam. Check the hooks at the same time to make sure that they still have a point.

Fly lines get dirty from general use. But they will also pick up bits of floating weed and, when you remove this weed, tiny bits of it will be left behind. You may not notice anything until you start retrieving line and feel a slight bump in an otherwise smooth line. You need to remove the little bits for a smooth retrieval – and remember, fly lines don't appreciate being trodden on

Fly lines

Fly lines get dirty through regular use without them being trodden on or dropped on the ground while casting and fishing. A dirty floating line will start to sink, and will also not cast very well. Fly lines have a slightly porous coating that releases any lubricants that were included during the manufacturing process. A dirty line will not release the lubricant because the pores will get clogged. Fly lines can be washed in warm water using hand soap or baby shampoo, but not washing-up liquid or any industrial cleaners which could damage the line. When you have washed the line, dry it thoroughly and then apply a thin coating of line dressing. You do this by putting a few drops of the dressing on a dry cloth or paper towel and then pulling the line through

One simple thing to do regularly that will help your casting is to clean your fly line and apply a special line dressing

163

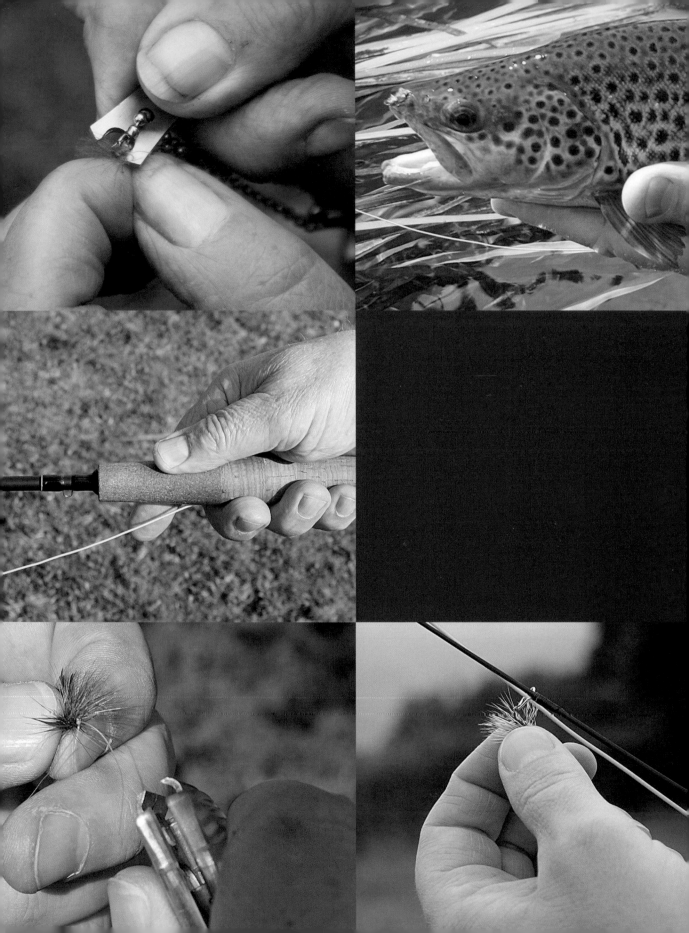

CHAPTER TWELVE

Essential fishing knots

It is important to be able to tie a few knots quickly and easily. Good knots should be easy to tie and they must work without slipping or coming undone at a key moment.

It is very important to be able to tie knots correctly and quickly. Fishing tackle cannot be put together without knots, as we have seen already, and tying flies to the tippet and changing flies through the course of a day's fishing are essential. A badly or incorrectly tied knot will slip, or break, and you may lose a fish and leave your fly in its mouth. It will pay big dividends if you spend

some time learning how to tie the knots that you will need at home, where you can sit and practise with plenty of light. Fortunately there is only one knot that you will have to tie frequently on the riverbank and that is the Eugene bend, although you may need to use the tucked half blood knot at times. You can practise tying knots using the eye in the end of a safety pin and a length of fly line. Don't try to save line, or mono, by trying to tie a knot too near the end – doing this will just make it more difficult to tie a good knot. If you have to cut the line and start again, you will not save any line.

Monofilament suitable for tippets is available in a wide range of strengths and thicknesses and from an equally wide range of manufacturers

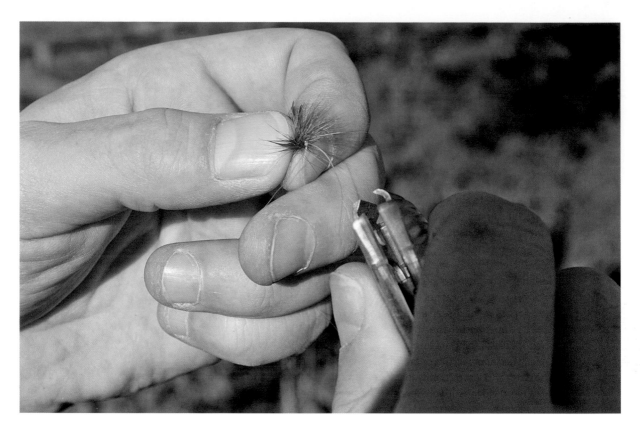

When you clip off the tag end of the tippet, make sure that you hold the tippet out of the way so that you cut the tag end and not the tippet itself. Don't drop lengths of tippet material or discarded tippets on the river bank as nylon can get tangled round the legs of birds and small mammals. Also, it does not biodegrade. Although you can chop unwanted nylon into very short lengths, it is much better to take it home with you and dispose of it safely in a dustbin, or burn it

In general, whenever you tie knots in mono-filament you need to wet the knot, which lubricates it and reduces friction, which otherwise creates heat which can damage the nylon. Knots should be drawn up with a single smooth tightening motion. This applies whether the monofilament is nylon, fluorocarbon, or any other monofilament polymer or copolymer.

The success of some knots depends on how many turns you make. Too few and the knot will slip; too many and you may not be able to tighten the knot properly, which will also cause it to fail. All the knots mentioned here are always tied with the same number of turns, regardless of the thickness of the material being used to tie them.

All knots should be trimmed so that they are neat and tidy. Tag ends that are not trimmed short

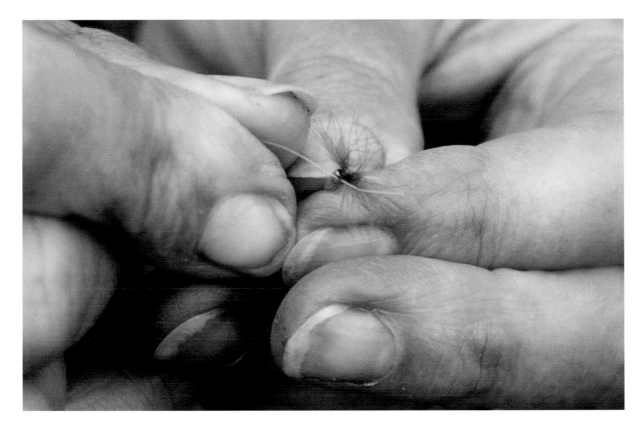

– no longer than ⅛ in (3 mm) – may catch pieces of weed or flotsam and can even cause a fish to reject your fly. Before trimming or cutting the waste or tag end of a knot, make sure that you are cutting the right piece. In fading light it is very easy to cut the wrong piece and end up having to tie the knot again.

On sunny days it can be difficult to see mono in bright sun, which makes threading the tippet through the eye of a hook difficult when tying-on or changing flies. To overcome this problem, turn your back to the sun so that you can thread the tippet in the shade.

A final piece of advice is not to rely on knots tied by other people. It is always best to tie your own knots. If one fails you have only yourself to blame.

Make sure that the eye of the hook is clear and that the end of the tippet has been cut cleanly before trying to tie on a new fly

Arbor knot

You use this knot to attach the end of the backing to the reel spool. It is not a knot that is used very often.

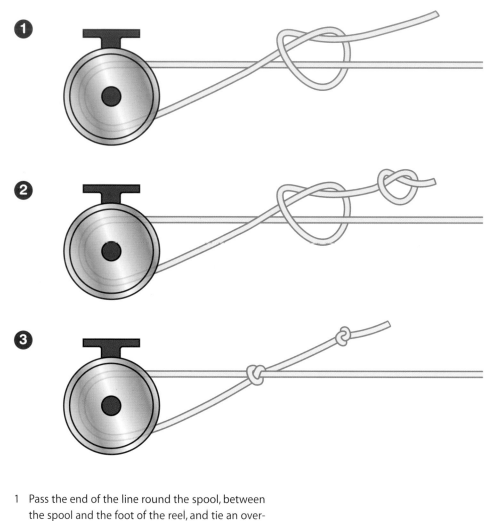

1 Pass the end of the line round the spool, between the spool and the foot of the reel, and tie an overhand knot, or thumb knot, round the running line.
2 Tie a second overhand knot in the tag end of the line. Tighten that knot and trim off any excess.
3 Now tighten the backing line and the first knot against the reel arbor. The knot on the tag end of the line acts as a stopper knot.

Tube nail knot

Although this knot was originally called the nail knot, it is much easier to tie using a piece of small diameter tube instead of a nail, hence the name tube nail knot. A piece of clean ballpoint pen ink tube or something similar is ideal.

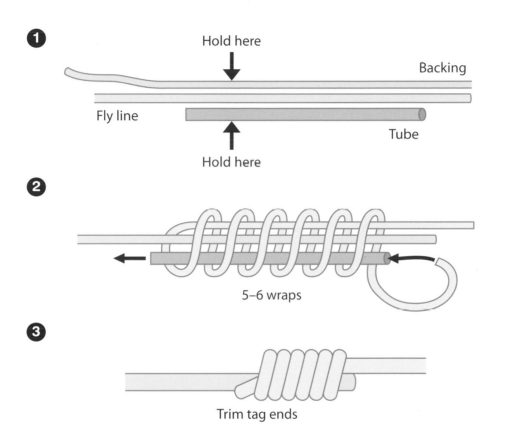

1 Hold here

Backing

Fly line

Tube

Hold here

2 5–6 wraps

3 Trim tag ends

1 Hold the tube and the end of the fly line, together, with your left thumb and forefinger, with the end of the fly line pointing to the right (if you are right-handed). Hold the backing with the end pointing to the left.

2 Wrap the end of the backing around the fly line and tube five or six times. Keep the turns as close together as possible and hold them with your thumb and finger.

3 Pull on the tag end of the backing to tighten the coils. Now insert the end of the backing through the tube.

4 Remove the tube (ensuring that the tag end of the backing is still accessible) and pull on both ends of the backing to tighten the knot, making sure that the coils lie close together. Don't let the loops formed at each end of the tube slide under the wraps.

5 Finish the knot by trimming the tag end of both backing and fly line. Test the knot by pulling firmly on both backing and line.

Eugene Bend

The Eugene bend is a strong, foolproof knot that is easy to tie and works best with monofilament lines of up to 12 lb (5.5 kg) breaking strain. It is one of the best knots to use to tie your fly to the end of the tippet. The knot is almost as strong as the breaking strain of the line – some knots provide less than one hundred per cent of the line strength and are best avoided. It is as foolproof as any fishing knot can be. It is no more wasteful than other knots for similar purposes. Because this knot is tied using monofilament only, it must be lubricated with saliva, or water, to make it slide easily and prevent friction causing heat which could damage the line. As you tighten the knot a slight click, or pop, tells you that the knot is set tight.

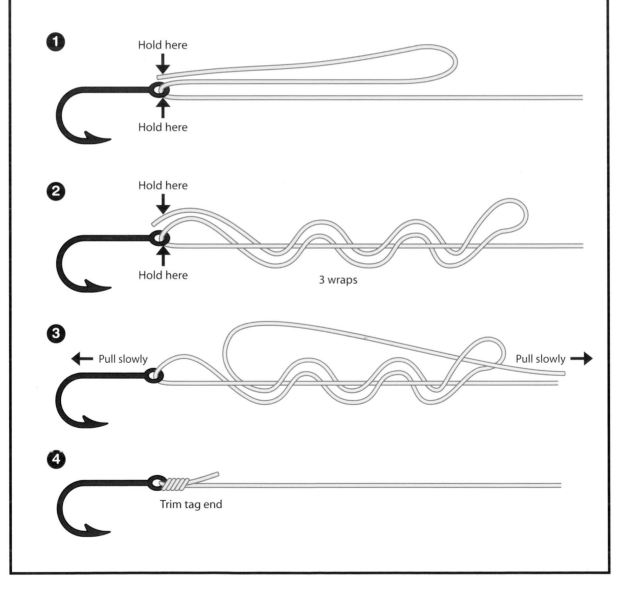

1 Hold here
Hold here

2 Hold here
Hold here
3 wraps

3 Pull slowly
Pull slowly

4 Trim tag end

Eugene Bend continued

1 Thread about 6 in (15 cm) of tippet through the hook eye, from the underside of the eye, and then run it back up alongside the standing main line.

2 Hold the two lines together with your thumb and finger and form a long loop by taking the tag end back towards the hook. Hold all the lines and hook eye between your thumb and index finger.

3 Wrap the loop you have just formed around the standing line three times.

4 Pass the tag end through the loop and then, using the finger and thumb of your right hand, pull the tag end until the knot is just snug – not tight – and the loops are small enough not to slip over the eye of the hook.

5 Wet the knot and pull slowly until the knot seats against the hook eye. When done correctly, you will feel and hear a reassuring slight click or 'pop' that tells you that the knot is tight. A properly tied and seated knot will have the tag end forming a very pronounced 'V' with the standing line.

6 Finish the knot by trimming the tag end. If you have limited use of your fingers, or your hands are very cold, this knot can be tied with the help of a pair of artery forceps, or a haemostat. To do this, insert a closed pair of forceps through the second loop (formed in stage 2 above) and rotate the ends of the forceps around the standing line three times. This wraps the second loop around the standing line the required three times. Then grasp the tag end of the tippet with your forceps and pull it through the second loop. When you have done this, you can complete the knot as above.

Tucked half blood knot

The tucked half blood knot is one of a number of knots used to attach a fly to the end of the tippet or the tippet to the ring on the end of a leader. The final tuck makes it a much more secure knot than the basic half blood knot. It works well for attaching a tippet to a ring, but is not as good as the Eugene bend for attaching a fly.

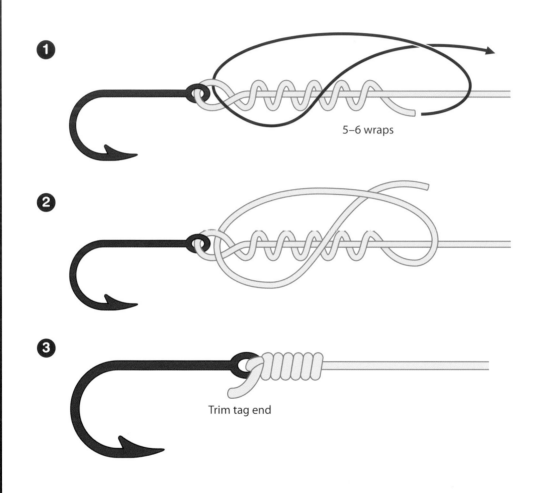

1

5–6 wraps

2

3

Trim tag end

1 Thread about 6 in (15 cm) of tippet through the eye of the hook, or the ring to which it is to be tied.
2 Keeping both parts of the line apart with your thumb and finger, wrap the tag end round the standing part five or six times.
3 Pass the tag end through the loop by the hook eye or ring.
4 Now pass the tag end through the loop that you have just formed. This is the tucked part of the knot.
5 Tighten the knot by moistening it and pulling on the standing part.
6 Finish the knot by trimming the tag end.

Loop-to-loop connection

The loop-to-loop connection is a knotless method of joining together two pieces of line, both with a loop tied on one end already.

1

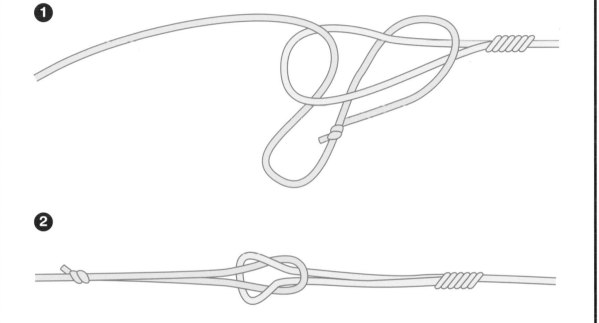

2

1 Pass the loop on the end of the line to be added over the end of the line to which you are adding a new length of line.
2 Now pass the end of the line being added through the loop on the end of the other line.
3 Pull it all the way through so that the loops come together.
4 Done correctly, the two loops should interlock to form a square knot.

Surgeon's knot

The surgeon's knot (sometimes known as a water knot) is easy and quick to tie and can be used to join together two lengths of monofilament of similar thickness, such as when adding a tippet to the end of a leader. You may sometimes hear this knot referred to as a two-turn water knot. It is only suitable for use when you are attaching a relatively short length of line, such as a tippet, as you have to pass one line through the loop you make. You can use this knot to create droppers when fishing a team of flies on stillwaters by increasing the lengths of line overlapped in stage 1.

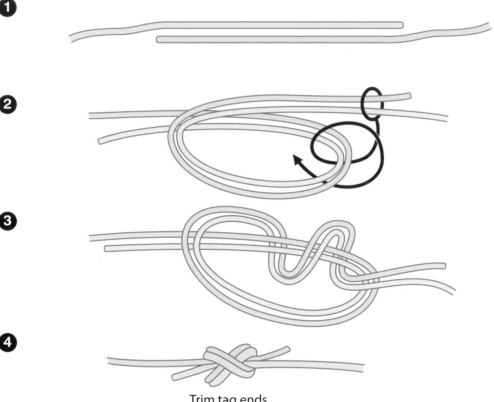

1

2

3

4

Trim tag ends

1 Lay the ends of the two pieces of line side by side so that they overlap by at least 4 in (10 cm).
2 Hold the long line and the end of the short line in one hand and use your other hand to form a loop with both lines.
3 Pass the ends of the lines through the loop, making an overhand loop.
4 Do the same thing again.

5 Tighten the knot by holding a pair of lines in each hand and moisten it before pulling.
6 Check that everything is tight by pulling the individual lines.
7 Complete the knot by trimming the tag ends. If you want a dropper, leave the end pointing away from the fly line long.

Surgeon's loop

The surgeon's loop is a good way to tie a loop on the end of a leader or tippet so that the two can be joined using the loop-to-loop connection. It is tied in a similar way to the surgeon's knot but uses only one length of monofilament.

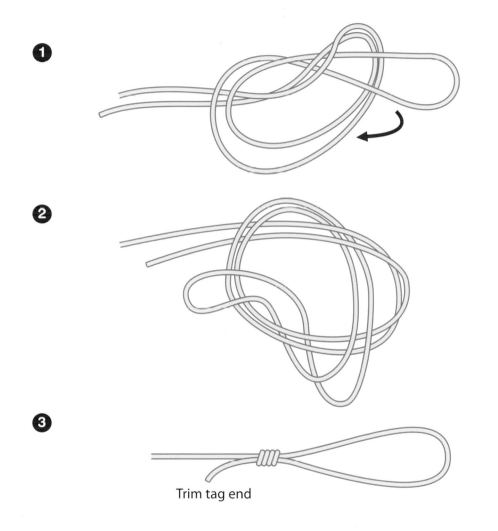

①

②

③

Trim tag end

1 Take about 4 in (10 cm) of the end of the line and use it to make a loop.
2 Hold the loop with one hand and use the other to tie an overhand knot with the two lines.
3 Pass the end of the loop through the loop you have just made.

4 Moisten the knot and, still holding the two lines in one hand, pass something smooth and round through the loop and pull firmly to tighten the knot.
5 Complete the knot by trimming the tag end.

CHAPTER THIRTEEN

How to tie a fly

Tying your own flies is an enjoyable and inter-esting pastime in itself. In fact some people started tying flies before learning to fish. Catching fish on flies that you have tied adds to the sense of achievement

Fly tying is a very good and pleasurable way to speed the passing of the closed season, which is often associated with dark winter evenings. Will you save money by tying your own flies? Probably not, but at least you will be sure that they are tied on good hooks – as long as you *do* buy good ones. It is all too easy to start building an enor-mous collection of tools and materials. You buy something that catches your eye one day and then find that you have never, or hardly ever, used it. Many items, particularly things synthetic, are often a different version of a well-known standard product, or a similar product with a different brand name. It is easy to be confused and find that you have bought the same thing but with a different name on the packet.

Like so much of fly fishing, fly tying involves building confidence in the materials that you are using and in what you are doing. I can still remember that when I started fly tying the hooks seemed so small and the tying thread broke as soon as I looked at it – or so it seemed. But once I had spent a little time breaking the thread I started to understand how strong it was and therefore how hard I could pull it. Then the day came when the hooks suddenly seemed to be that much bigger and the tying thread was too thick. Confidence is very important and the only way you can develop it is by trying, making mistakes and trying again until things start to fall into place. And they will, given a little time.

At first it is very difficult to appreciate how little material you need when tying a fly – for example, dubbing. Obviously if tying-in a hackle you have to use one feather, but even then some flies need very few turns of hackle, perhaps no more than two or possibly three. And over-dressed flies with too many turns of hackle just

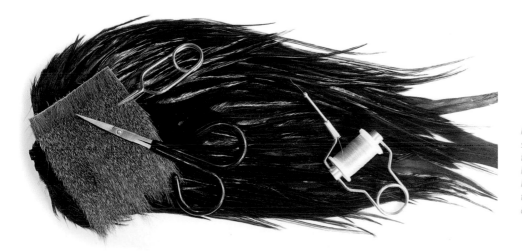

Hackles and hair, a sharp pair of scissors, tying thread, a bobbin holder and a pair of hackle pliers are some of the essential materials and tools used by fly tiers

A simple vice with a pedestal base that will hold a range of sizes of hooks. The jaws can be rotated so that you can look at the fly in the round as you tie it

do not look right. When using dubbing, start by taking a pinch and then take just half of that first pinch. It is better to start with too little than too much because if you have too little you can always add a bit more. For a finished fly to look right it is very important to get the proportions correct. Over-fat bodies made with too much dubbing look clumsy and wrong. Hackles that are too long in the fibre for the size of hook spoil a fly's proportions as can too many turns of hackle. Unless a fly dressing specifies longer tails, tails want to be between half the length and the length of the hook shank.

Good lighting is essential and having a white board, or sheet of card, on your tying table also helps by reflecting light, and the tools and materials on it will be easier to see. If you spend a lot of time outdoors and find that rough bits of skin catch or snag your thread, use some hand cream before starting tying as this will help smooth your skin.

Essential tools and equipment

SCISSORS

A really good pair of scissors with very sharp, fine-pointed blades is one of the most important items of equipment. Suitable scissors are available with either straight or curved blades. As well as choosing scissors with short, very sharp and fine blades, check to make sure that the finger holes are the right size for your fingers: if your fingers are a tight fit, it makes putting the scissors down when you don't want to use them more difficult. If you have only one pair, make sure that you cut thick hackles and wire at the thick end of the blades, preserving the fine tips for very small, fine materials and thread. Keep your scissors sharp and look after them.

VICE

Although anglers and professional fly tiers were making, or dressing, flies before fly-tying vices had been invented, today a vice is essential. Vices are available in a wide range of styles and, inevitably, prices. Obviously a vice must hold hooks firmly so that they will not slip, and without damaging them. Vices are made either to be fixed to the edge of a table or desk with a G-clamp, or with a pedestal base. The latter is to be preferred as it does away with the need to be able to clamp the vice to a table (which may mean that the vice is too close to you) and you can move it about if you want to during operations. Most pedestals are very heavy, which is unnecessary, as it is the area of the pedestal that counts. Some of the cheap vices leave quite a lot to be desired when it comes to ease of use and general efficiency.

DESK LIGHT

Good light concentrated on the tying vice is vital. Inexpensive halogen desk lights work well as they can be positioned and adjusted to deliver the light in the right place, with the lamp itself out of the way. There are also fly-tying lights made that fit to the stem of the vice.

BOBBIN HOLDER

A bobbin holder is used to carry a spool of tying thread and dispense the thread through a very fine, preferably ceramic or ceramic-lined, tube. The tube must be very smooth so that it does not cut the tying thread. The bobbin holds the spool under pressure, either with springy arms or, on more expensive models, an adjustable drag system. The weight of the bobbin and spool will keep the tying thread under tension when you need to let go of it. If you decide that your first purchase can be improved, don't worry about replacing it with a better one as an extra bobbin holder can be useful (you can keep different-coloured threads ready for action).

HACKLE PLIERS

Hackle pliers are used to hold materials, such as feathers, that are wound round the hook shank to form the hackle. They are made of spring steel and need to hold a slippery feather firmly. Some are fitted with rubber-covered jaws. Efficient but inexpensive hackle pliers can be bought with a spring-loaded push clip (an idea borrowed from the electronics industry) with or without a large finger ring. A heavy pair, as well as a light pair, will be useful for tensioning the end of the tying thread when it breaks. As with bobbin holders, you will probably end up with more than one pair of hackle pliers.

DUBBING NEEDLE

A dubbing needle is a fine needle with a handle that is used to pick out dubbing, or clear the eye of a hook of foreign matter, and for applying varnish to the heads of flies.

DUBBING WAX

Although tying thread is pre-waxed, you will still need to add a little wax to it to help the dubbing stick to the thread.

WHIP-FINISH TOOL

The heads of flies are usually finished by making a whip finish with the tying thread between the front of the hackle and the back of the eye of the hook. This can be done with your fingers (see page 182) but a whip-finish tool can make the operation easier. There are three styles of tool available. Each one is used in a slightly different way, although the end result is the same: a perfect whip finish. Although they are supplied with instructions, there are many videos on using each style on YouTube. Seeing one in action is very much better and easier than trying to understand inadequate written instructions. This really is a case of the cliché 'a picture is worth a thousand words'.

SUPERGLUE

Superglue is useful for fixing lead wire, used to weight nymphs, in place on the hook shank as well as securing broken tying thread.

Some essential materials

HOOKS

You will need a range of types and sizes of hooks, suitable for tying dry flies and nymphs. Beware buying 'bargain' hooks as they can often be useless: they either break or bend because they have not been tempered properly. Bad hooks will lose you a lot of fish. If you tie a nice fly and hook a fish with it, the last thing you want is to lose the fish because the hook has broken or straightened out. Hook-makers produce a number of all- or general-purpose hooks, some in different weights of wire, that will be suitable for tying a wide range of flies. Hooks made from heavier wire are better for tying nymphs as you want them to sink. Conversely, the best dry-fly hooks are made from very fine wire. More companies are now producing barbless hooks that make releasing fish much quicker and easier. Suggested sizes are 12, 14, 16 and 18.

HOW FISH HOOKS ARE MADE

Some of the names of the styles and bends of hooks that originated from either the inventor's name or the places that they were made are still in use today. Hook-making has gone from a cottage industry, based in Redditch, England, to a high-tech industry centred in Japan and the Far East. Production of fish hooks began in Redditch in about 1770 when needle-makers started making hooks as they required the same methods and skills needed to make needles. Then, in 1803, Polycarp Allcock, an apprentice hook-maker, started his own hook-making business. It was his son, Samuel, who developed the business which, by 1880, claimed to be the world's largest manufacturer of fishing tackle. The success and development of hook-making depended on the supply of high-quality steel, although the quality of hooks remained very variable. In addition to Redditch, which had seventeen firms making hooks by 1823, hook-makers were to be found in Kendal and in Dublin and Limerick in Ireland.

The production of fish hooks was carried out by a cottage industry that sent out batches of needles to families for bending into hooks. One of the problems affecting the quality of early fish hooks was the way that barbs were made. This was done by cutting the wire and, if the cut was made too deep, then the hook would be likely to break at the barb. Batch tempering was not a completely reliable process and fishermen became proficient at recognizing soft hooks which tended to be light-blue in colour instead of purple blue.

Until very near the end of the nineteenth century virtually all hooks were 'blind' – they had no eye. In order that a hook could be attached to the end of a fly line, first a length of gut was whipped to the hook shank before the fly was tied, and later gut loops were used. It may seem extraordinary today to learn that the introduction of eyed hooks was not an instant success. H.S. Hall was experimenting with making eyed hooks in the 1870s and, in August 1879, he met one George Selwyn Marryat, the pre-eminent Victorian fly fisherman. Marryat, who had fished with eyed hooks earlier in the decade, possibly as much as six years before he met Hall, gave him much practical assistance, which enabled Hall to perfect what were then the smallest eyed hooks. The eyed hook was probably the most important development in fly fishing in the Victorian era. Without the availability of small-eyed, fine wire hooks, it is arguable that Marryat, Hall and F.M. Halford would not have been able to develop dry-fly fishing the way that they did.

The mass-production of high-quality, reliable fish hooks was made possible by the introduction of an automatic fish hook machine. This was invented by Mathias Topp soon after he joined the Norwegian firm Mustad in 1877. In essence Topp's machine allowed steel wire to be fed in at one end and hooks to come out at the other. In America, claims have been made that Dr Chauncey O. Crosby of the American Fish Hook & Needle Co., founded in 1864, invented the first automated hook-making machine.

Today, fish hooks are made from premium grade high-carbon steel, free from impurities, which eliminates faults in the metal that could weaken a hook. Two crucial aspects of hook-making are tempering hooks and then sharpening them. Each hook is tempered by heating it to a specific temperature for that particular style and size, and then cooling it in oil to produce a hook that is very strong but not brittle. And no hook is any good unless it is really sharp.

Traditionally, fishing hooks were sharpened through a process known as mechanical sharpening, similar to sharpening a knife on a stone. Although it was effective, the process left the hook with minor imperfections. Today, hooks are sharpened chemically using a process similar to the one that has been used for surgical needles for many years. Chemical sharpening involves the mechanically sharpened hook being submerged in an acid that smoothes or 'eats away' the metal and produces a refined point. It is a critical operation because if a hook is left in the chemical for too long it may dull the point and weaken the barb. Done correctly, hook points will be as smooth and sharp as possible.

TYING THREADS

Do not buy very fine tying thread when you first start tying flies as it will break far too easily. When you have built up some confidence, then you can think about buying thinner threads. Threads are sold pre-waxed so that they do not have to be waxed before use, except when using dubbing materials. (The wax helps the thread grip other materials.) Beige or olive are good neutral colours that will blend with most tying materials to start with, although black and red are useful to have. You can colour-code your flies by, for example, using red thread to tie weighted nymphs and black for unweighted flies.

FINE BRASS AND COPPER WIRES

These wires will be used to rib fly bodies and, in the case of the pheasant tail nymph, to tie and weight the fly as it uses no conventional tying thread.

LEAD WIRE

Lead wire is used to weight nymphs to make them sink. It is available on small spools in a range of diameters to suit different sizes of hook. It is better to buy a spool of fine wire as this will be less bulky on small hooks, but when you want more weight you can simply wrap on more wire.

BEADS

Beads are available in copper and brass, in a range of sizes to suit your hook sizes. Tungsten beads can be used to add extra weight to flies. Some are sold by name i.e. small, medium or large, or by diameter: 2 mm or 2.5 mm.

VARNISH

Although special fly-tying varnishes – sometimes known as head cement – are available, many fly tiers use women's clear nail varnish.

HACKLES AND HAIR

Hackles, as the feathers fly tiers use are known, are, in the main, the result of genetic selective breeding. The result is very high-quality and extremely long feathers which can each be used to tie a number of flies. Hackles are sold as whole or half cock saddles, or capes (or necks); a half saddle is a sensible purchase. It is also possible to buy packets of loose feathers specially selected and sized for a particular hook size or range of sizes; these are good if you do not want to invest in a whole or half saddle or cape. Although genetic hackles are expensive to buy, they are much better than cheaper Chinese or Indian feathers because they are of a much higher and more consistent quality. This makes them much easier to tie with. Cock hackles are used for dry flies as they are stiffer than hen hackles so they float better and higher on the water. The most useful hackles to buy are grizzle, or grizzly, (black and white barred feathers), black and ginger. Also useful to have are some cock pheasant central tail feathers. These can be bought, acquired from a shooting friend or even found on the side of roads.

Roadkill – dead birds and animals – can be a source of supply of grey squirrels, rabbits and the occasional hare. A hare's mask and ears are the source of dubbing for hare's ear nymphs, and fibres for tails of flies. Although an elk would be an unlikely roadside find in Britain, a piece of elk body hair is very useful for dry fly tails and the wings of a number of patterns. It can be bought either as natural or bleached.

DUBBING

A wide range of dubbing can be bought in special dispenser boxes with an assortment of twelve colours, each in its own compartment – or you can acquire a hare's mask and a piece of hare body fur. A box of hare dubbing in muted colours, including natural, and a box of synthetic dry fly dubbing will be enough to get you started.

Getting started

When you are all set up and ready to start tying, place a hook in your vice and then flick the hook with your finger. If it is a sound hook it will make a ping as you flick it. If it has not been tempered enough, it may bend or, if it is too brittle, it might even break. Some fly tiers maintain that when you put a hook in your vice, you should not cover the hook point and barb as this will damage them – instead you should leave them exposed. The problem with this for a beginner is that it is very easy to nick your finger on the exposed point or cut the thread at a crucial stage of the process. It is probably better to just cover the point of the hook with the jaws of the vice. Don't over-tighten the vice on the hook; it wants to be tight enough so that the hook does not move but not so tight that you risk damaging it.

Before starting trying to tie an actual fly, spend some time practising tying the thread on the hook and covering the hook shank in touching turns. Doing this will give you a feeling for how hard you can pull the thread before it breaks and, with care, you will have fewer breaks when tying a fly.

With a hook in the vice you need to thread your bobbin holder. To do this, place a spool of tying thread between its arms and pull off a short length of thread. Cut the end of the thread to make sure it is clean and then poke it into the tube and suck on the other end of the tube; this should pull the thread through.

As you work your way through to the end of tying a fly you will need to cut different things. If the fly has a hackle you will need to cut the end of the hackle and then the tying thread. If you use your scissors in the normal way you risk cutting unwanted hackle fibres, or even the thread. Instead, hold the item that you want to cut firmly and push the opened blades of the scissors against it. It doesn't require much pressure to sever the stalk of a hackle or the tying thread. Doing this will ensure that only the part of the hackle, or thread, under tension will be cut.

WHEN THE THREAD BREAKS

Tying thread breaks because you pull it too hard or you cut it on the exposed hook point. When it breaks, don't panic. Clip a pair of hackle pliers – the heavier the better – onto the end of the thread attached to the fly. If the thread breaks close to the hook, unravel a turn or two of thread so that you have something to which to attach the hackle pliers. The hackle pliers will keep tension on the thread while you cut the end of

the thread on the spool and re-thread the bobbin holder. This is much easier to do with thread with a 'clean' end. Take the bobbin holder with a length of thread exposed and tie on, as you did at the start, and make sure that you make four or five turns over the cut/broken thread as well as the end of the thread that you are tying on. Take hold of both the broken thread and the new spare end and trim both close to the hook shank. You can add a spot of superglue or head cement for extra security.

PINCH AND LOOP METHOD

The best way to tie-in the various materials is to use what is called the pinch and loop method. Using a pinch and loop will ensure that the materials are tied-in on top of the hook shank and not on one side. To use this method, hold the tail fibres, or body material, with the first finger and thumb of your non-thread hand (the left hand if you are right-handed) and then position your finger and thumb on top of the hook shank, which you then pinch, holding the materials in place. Raise the thread up between your thumb and the nearside of the hook shank at the point at which you want to tie-in the fibres. Pinch everything firmly while you pass the bobbin and thread over the far side of the hook shank. As you pass it down the far side of the hook, take the thread under your finger, making sure that there is a loop of thread sticking up. Now pass the thread back up under your thumb and pull the thread up to tighten everything. Then repeat the process. You can now move your fingers and the tails, or material, will be held firmly in the correct place and position.

MAKING A WHIP FINISH

A whip finish is made by making four or five turns of a loop of tying thread over the loose end of the thread, which is then pulled tight and cut off. Once you have acquired the knack, it is a simple procedure. Start by making a loop with the tying thread; insert your first and second fingers into the loop, at the same time as maintaining tension on the loose end of the thread with your other hand and holding it alongside the hook shank.

You can use the second finger to push the thread into the 'V' formed by the thread and the hook shank.

Now take the first turn with the open loop of thread around the hook shank, keeping the thread under tension by revolving your first finger around the hook. Make sure that the loose end of the thread (and the bottom of the loop) does not get pulled round the hook shank. As your fingers come up in front of the hook to complete the first turn, you will have to change the position of your fingers so that the second finger holds the bottom part of the loop in the right position. Repeat the whole procedure another three or four times, depending on how much space you have got available.

To complete the whip finish, hold the loop tight with one finger at the same time as drawing the end of the thread through the wraps that you have just made until it is tight. Finally, cut away the spare thread as close as possible against the whip finish.

It's time to tie a fly

There is a convention in fly tying that all the materials in fly dressings are listed in the order in which they are to be tied. Check the dressing and make sure that you have got everything to hand before getting underway.

TYING A PHEASANT TAIL DRY FLY
Hook: Light wire dry fly, size 14, 16, 18
Thread: Black
Tail: Honey dun cock hackle fibres, or three fibres from cock pheasant tail feather
Body: Two or three fibres from cock pheasant tail feather
Rib: Fine gold wire
Hackle: Honey dun cock

All the materials and tools – apart from a vice and hooks – that you need to tie a pheasant tail dry fly

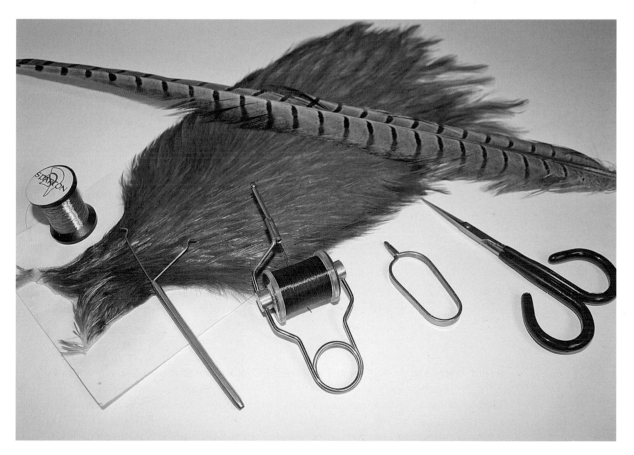

Step 3 – Pick up your bobbin holder and pull off about 5 in (12.5 cm) of thread with your other hand. Still holding the end of the thread tightly, pass it round the hook shank, just behind the eye and, holding the thread horizontal, wrap the thread (away from you) round the hook shank, and over the end you are holding, two or three times to secure the thread. Change the position of your hand, holding the end of the thread so that it is directly over the hook shank, and the thread is at an angle of forty-five degrees, and continue to wrap the tying thread all the way along the hook shank. Holding the end of the thread at an angle will help each successive turn slide down the slope against its neighbour in what are known as touching turns. What you are trying to do is to cover the hook shank from just behind the eye to the point where the bend starts with a complete and even layer, or bed, of thread; the rest of the fly is built on this foundation. Be careful not to break the thread by applying too much tension, and also watch out for the point of the hook (if it is not covered by your vice) as you approach the bend: you can easily nick the tying thread or a finger. Cut off the spare end of the thread a couple of turns before where you need to start making the body, to ensure that you cover the cut end. The better the foundation, the better the finished fly.

Below Once the tying thread is secured to the hook shank, hold the spare end at an angle to the hook shank and wrap the thread towards the bend of the hook in even touching turns

Step 1 – Take a spool of tying thread of the specified colour, place it in the bobbin holder and thread it.

Step 2 – Select a hook of the required size and fix it in your vice. Then flick the eye of the hook to make sure that it is not going to bend or break.

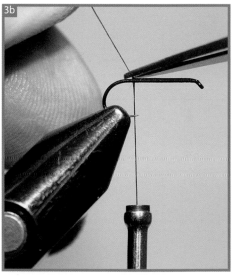

Cut away the spare end of the thread a couple of turns before where you will start making the body of the fly

Step 4 – Now that you have tied the thread foundation, leave the thread hanging while you select
and remove five or six fibres from a honey dun
cock hackle. Do this by stroking the fibres so that
they stand out from the hackle stalk and then cut
or pluck them off. Alternatively, you can use two
or three fibres from a cock pheasant tail feather
(as per the body in Step 7).

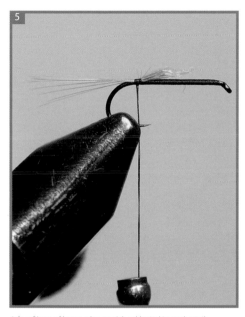

A few fibres of honey dun cock hackle tied in as the tail

Step 5 – Tie-in the tail so that the fibres are a little
shorter than the length of the hook shank. The
best way to tie-in the various materials is to use
the pinch and loop method described above.
Using a pinch and loop will ensure that the materials are tied-in on top of the hook shank and not
on one side. Hold the fibres with the first finger
and thumb of your non-thread hand (the left
hand if you are right-handed) so that you cover
the length you want for the tail, and then position
your finger and thumb on top of the hook shank
which you then pinch, holding the tail fibres in
place.

Step 6 – With the tail in place, still secured by just
two turns of thread, take your spool of fine gold
wire and cut off a short length. This will be used to
rib the body.

Step 7 – Cut two or three long fibres from one side
of a cock pheasant tail feather. Then take your
piece of wire and the pheasant fibres and hold
them so that the end of the wire and the tips of the
fibres are all even. Tying-in the fibres by the tips
means that you will be able to tie a smoother body.
You now need to tie them in at the same place as
you tied-in the tail. To do this you need the fibres
and wire to be a little shorter than the hook shank.
Use the pinch and loop method again, but this
time make sure that the ribbing wire is underneath
the hook shank and the body fibres are on top. If
you are happy, wrap some more turns of thread
over the tail fibres, ribbing wire and body fibres.
Continue wrapping forward to the point where
you tied-in the thread at the start. If the wire or any
fibres are too long then snip off the excess. Leaving
everything long and covering with tying thread
will produce a smoother body.

*Pheasant tail feather
fibres and ribbing wire
tied in ready to make the
body. Don't tie in the
body fibres too close to
the tips as they may
break when you try to
wrap them round the
hook shank. Leaving the
tips long helps produce a
smooth body*

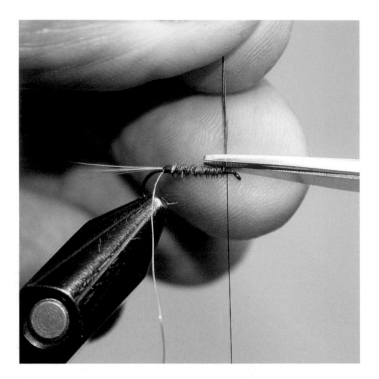

Wrap the tail feather fibres forward and then secure with turns of tying thread. Then cut away the surplus as close as you can

spaced you can make the turns of wire the better the fly will look. Wrapping the rib in the opposite direction from the body fibres prevents it from being hidden by the body material, as well as providing extra security for the fibres.

Step 10 – The last item to be tied in is the hackle. This is best done by tying it in by the stalk which is much stronger than the tip. If you have bought a pack of loose hackles take one that is the right size for the hook on which you are tying your fly. Before you can tie it in, you must prepare it properly. Hold the feather in one hand and, with the other, stroke the fibres at the end of the stalk so that they stand out. If there are any soft, webby fibres cut them off with your scissors so that you are left with long, straight fibres. Cut off of any excess stalk and then cut away the fibres on both sides of the stalk for about 2 mm. What you want are a few fibre ends standing out from the central stalk. These short fibres will help secure the hackle when you tie it in.

Step 8 – To make the body of the fly, take hold of the ends of the pheasant fibres with a pair of hackle pliers and then wrap them close together forwards round the hook shank in the same direction as the tying thread, and stop when you reach the point where you started the fly. The body must stop a couple of millimetres behind the eye of the hook so that you have somewhere to add the hackle and make a whip finish head to complete the fly. Secure the ends of the fibres with a couple of turns of thread and then cut away the spare material. Sometimes it can be easier to hold the fibres with the finger and thumb of your thread hand and, as you make each turn, you can keep the fibres under tension by pressing them against the hook shank with the first finger of your other hand.

Step 9 – Complete the body by winding the ribbing wire in three or four evenly spaced spirals (the exact number depends on the length of the hook shank, but they want to be a bit under 2 mm apart), in the opposite direction to the fibres, and secure the end with two or three turns of thread, before cutting off the excess. The more evenly

The prepared hackle has been tied in and is now ready to be wrapped around the hook shank

Step 11 – To tie-in the hackle, hold it with your free hand, with the good, shiny side of the feather uppermost and the stem facing down and towards the eye. Make three firm turns around the hackle stem and hook. Cut off any excess hackle stem and wind the thread forward to just behind the eye.

Step 12 – The next task is to wind the hackle around the hook. To do this, grasp the tip of the feather with a pair of hackle pliers and make the first turn against the end of the body, followed by two more turns, one in front of the other. Hold the hackle on top of the shank and secure it with three tight turns. When tying-off the hackle, try to hold back the individual fibres of the feather with the finger and thumb of one hand and then 'wobble' the tying thread from side to side as you take it round the hook shank. Doing this helps to prevent trapping individual fibres. Still holding the feather firmly, remove the excess by pushing your opened scissors against the feather. Make sure that you do not cut the tying thread at the same time.

Step 13 – To complete the tying you need to make a neat whipped head to which you apply a little varnish or head cement. This secures the hackle as well as making a head for the fly. Be sparing with the varnish as you do not want to use so much that it fills the eye of the hook. If that does happen, you can clear the eye by passing a pheasant tail fibre through it, pointed end first.

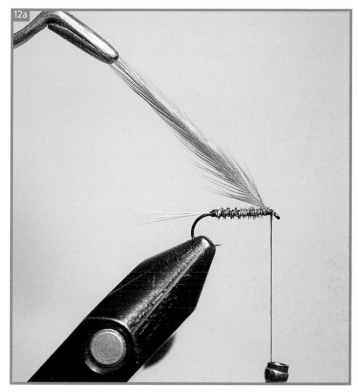

Hold the end of the hackle with a pair of hackle pliers and make three turns around the hook

Secure the hackle with three turns of tying thread and then cut away the excess hackle as neatly as possible

The finished fly

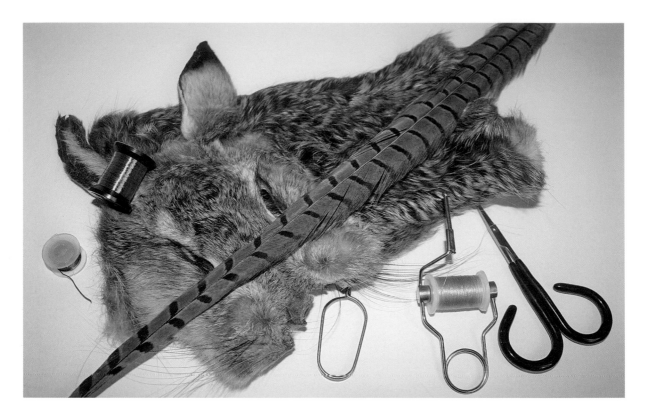

All the materials and tools – apart from a vice and hooks – that you need to tie a gold-ribbed hare's ear nymph

TYING A GOLD-RIBBED HARE'S EAR NYMPH

Hook: Nymph or wet fly, size 12, 14, 16
Thread: Beige or olive
Weight: Lead wire
Tail: Hare's body fur
Rib: Gold wire

Body: Hare's ear dubbing
Thorax: Hare's ear dubbing picked out with a dubbing needle to suggest legs
Wing case: Two or three dark cock pheasant tail feather fibres

Step 1 – Lay out all the materials that you will need on your tying bench so that everything is to hand.

Step 2 – Put a spool of thread in the bobbin holder and thread it.

Step 3 - Take a hook of the required type and size, fix it in your vice and then flick the hook eye to make sure that it is tempered correctly and is not going to bend or break.

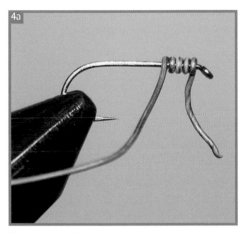

Wrap four turns of lead wire onto the shank of the hook. A spot of superglue will hold it in place. You can make lighter or heavier flies by using fewer or more turns of wire

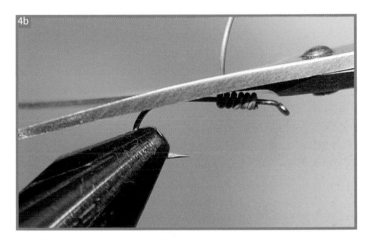

Cut the lead wire with the bottom end of the blades of the scissors. Use the tips for threads and hackles only

Step 4 – Wrap four turns of lead wire round the hook shank just behind the hook eye. Smooth down the ends against the hook shank.

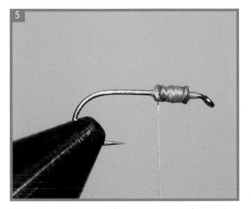

Smoothing down the ends of the lead wire with a fingernail is easier if the wire is glued in place. Now wrap all the turns with tying thread to hold the wire in place just clear of the back of the eye of the hook

Step 5 - Take hold of your bobbin holder and pull off about 5 in (12.5 cm) of thread with your other hand. Still holding the end of the thread tightly, pass it round the hook shank, between the eye and the lead wire, and, holding the end of the thread horizontally, wrap the thread (away from you) round the hook shank and over the end you are holding two or three times to secure the thread. Now wrap the thread backwards and forwards over the lead wire to hold it in place, making sure that it does not slide forwards too close to the eye of the hook. You need to leave a space of about 2 mm between the lead and the eye of the hook. Once you have secured the lead in place, wrap the tying thread along the hook shank in touching turns to the start of the bend. Cut off the spare end of the thread a couple of turns before where you need to start making the body and ensure that you cover the cut end.

Step 6 – Leave the thread hanging and cut about 4 in (10 cm) of fine gold wire for the rib.

A pinch of hairs tied in for the tail

Step 7 – Take a small pinch of long hairs from a hare's mask or a piece of body fur for the tail, which should be quite short. You can measure them against the shank so the tail will be about half a shank's length long. Before tying-in the tail, remove the soft under-fur. Hold the hair with the thick ends together, and tie in using a pinch and loop, followed by the ribbing wire. Continue wrapping the thread forwards to the back of the lead wire, to cover everything evenly and smoothly. Trim off any excess material.

The gold ribbing wire has been added

Step 8 – Take the thread back to the tail of the fly in well-spaced open turns. (You are simply moving your thread from one end of the fly to the other.) An alternative is to tie-in the tail fibres by themselves and wrap over the exposed ends forwards to the back of the lead wire. At this point you can hold the ribbing wire alongside the hook shank, catch-in the end and then wrap back to the tail. With the thread back at the tail end of the fly you are ready to dub the body. The body wants to be carrot-shaped, gradually swelling towards the thorax.

Applying dubbing wax to the tying thread helps the fur used to make the dubbed body adhere to the thread

Apply the dubbing very sparingly at first as you can always add a little more if necessary. Too much dubbing will produce a clumsy-looking fly

Wind the dubbed thread forwards in tight, even turns

Step 9 – To make a dubbed body, apply some dubbing wax, sparingly, to about 2 in (5 cm) of tying thread, the wax will help the hare dubbing to stick to the thread. Take a very small pinch of dubbing and divide it in half. It is better to start with very little, as it is quite easy to add more if needed. Spread it out thinly along the length of waxed thread. Let the thread and bobbin hang over the first finger of your left hand (if right-handed) while you roll the dubbing on and around the thread in one direction. You are trying to make a hairy rope, with the dubbing spread evenly along it. Now wind the dubbed thread along the body, making sure that the first turn covers where the tail is tied in, as far forwards as the back of the lead wire. Remove any unused dubbing from the thread.

The fibres for the thorax cover have been tied in and the dubbing taken forward over the lead wire

Step 10 – Next, cut two or three fibres from a cock pheasant tail feather which you are going to tie-in just behind the lead wire as the thorax cover. Tie them in by the thick ends.

Step 11 – Wax a short length thread and apply a little dubbing. You use this to cover the lead wire, creating the nymph's thorax.

Rib the body with the gold wire and then tie off firmly

Step 12 – Wind the wire rib forwards in evenly spaced turns but in the opposite direction from the dubbed body. Secure the end of the wire, with a few turns of tying thread, and cut off the surplus wire.

The thorax cover is in place and the surplus fibres can be removed. All that is needed to finish the fly is a to make a neat whip-finish and add a drop of varnish

Step 13 – Pull the pheasant fibres forwards over the thorax and tie down behind the eye of the hook. To make a slightly more pronounced wing case, bend the fibres back over the thorax, tie them at the rear of the thorax and then bring them forward again and tie off. Trim away the excess and complete the tying by making a neat whip-finish. Don't forget to apply a little varnish to the head.

Step 14 – You can pick out the dubbing on the thorax with a dubbing needle to accentuate the nymph's legs.

The finished fly. When tying flies it is very easy to concentrate on making the side of the fly that you can see look nice and to forget about the other side. You need to remember to rotate your vice once in a while and check that the other side is looking good too

CHAPTER FOURTEEN

What does that mean?

Fly fishing, like many sports, has its own lexicon of seemingly incomprehensible words. Here are plain English definitions of the most common words and phrases that you are likely to encounter.

Action A word used to describe the feel, the way and how much a rod bends while casting. Actions can be slow or full flex, mid- or through-action, and fast or tip-action. Different rod-makers use varying terms to describe rod action. A slow or full flex rod bends for most of its length, whereas a fast or tip-action rod flexes predominantly towards the tip.

Arbor The centre, or axle, of a fly reel, but also used to refer to the removable spool which holds the fly line and **backing**. Reel spools, or arbors, are referred to as standard (which tend to be narrow as well as of smaller diameter), or medium or large arbor, which are both larger in diameter and wider. A large arbor reel stores the line in bigger coils than a standard arbor and the effective diameter of the spool remains more constant.

Arbor knot Knot used to attach the end of the backing to the centre of the reel spool, or **arbor**.

Back cast The part of a cast made when the fly line goes behind the angler. *See also* **Forward cast**.

Backing Thin line used to increase the diameter of the spool, or **arbor**, of a reel and to provide extra line should a powerful fish run further than the length of a fly line.

Balanced A word applied to tackle to describe when the rod, reel and line are all working in harmony.

Bank Riverbanks are named when looking downstream, when the true right-hand bank is on the right and the true left-hand bank to the left.

Barbless hook A hook made without a barb so that a fish can be unhooked quickly and easily. On hooks with barbs, the barb can be flattened with a pair of pliers or forceps.

Bead head An artificial fly fitted with a glass or metal bead often, but not always, immediately behind the eye of the hook.

Beat A stretch of river, or riverbank, available to be fished by one or more anglers.

Blank The carbon-fibre tube that forms the basis of a rod. It is turned into a finished rod when various fittings and components are added.

Bobbin holder A device used to hold a spool of thread under tension when tying flies.

Bulger A fish that when it is feeding on nymphs on or just below the surface causes the surface of the water to move or 'bulge' upwards.

Butt The thick part of the leader. The butt of a leader is attached to the fly line. Can also refer to the bottom section of a fly rod.

Cape Hackles from the neck of a bird used for tying flies. *See also* **Saddle**.

Casting arc The path that the tip of a fly rod follows during a complete cast.

Casting knots Knots that form in the tippet or leader through bad or faulty casting. Known popularly, but inaccurately, as wind knots.

Casting loop The loop formed at the end of a back cast or forward cast as the line unrolls and straightens. Loops can be narrow (good) or wide (less good). *See also* **Tailing loop**.

Catch and release Often referred to as C & R. The process of releasing fish, rather than landing them and killing them. On a catch-and-release fishery it is illegal to kill any fish. Fish that are being released should be handled as little as possible. The use of barbless hooks is usually encouraged. *See also* **Long distance release** and **Barbless hooks**.

Dead drift When a dry fly moves at the same speed and direction as the surface current, or a nymph moves at the same speed and direction as the sub-surface current as though it is not attached to anything. Usually applied to casting and fishing your fly so that it achieves a dead drift. *See also* **Drag-free drift**.

Dipping point The point at which the nymph fisher's leader cuts through the surface of the water. Any change in movement or attitude may indicate that a fish has taken your fly below the surface.

Double haul A way of increasing line speed, by pulling on the line while casting, to increase the length of cast.

Double taper A standard fly line design in which both ends of the line are tapered evenly while the greater portion or 'belly' of the line is level or untapered. Either end can be used.

Downstream The direction in which a river is flowing. *See also* **Upstream**.

Drag, or dragging A fly is said to be dragging when it is moving faster or slower than the current or in other unnatural ways. This can often cause a disturbance of the surface of the water. Flies fished below the surface can also cause drag. Usually a bad thing except when fishing a skating caddis on the surface.

Drag-free drift A perfect float in which the fly travels at the same speed as the current. Used for both dry-fly and nymph fishing and results from making and fishing a cast without creating any drag. *See also* **Dead drift**.

Drag system A simple click system, or a system of discs, designed to prevent a reel spool from over-running when line is stripped from it quickly and to provide resistance when line is pulled off the reel.

Drop, on the A term used to describe when fish in stillwaters take a nymph or wet fly as it sinks after being cast.

Dropper A short length of tippet material attached to, or forming part of, a leader to which a dropper fly is attached when fishing with more than one fly. It can also be a fly and length of monofilament attached directly to the hook bend of the point fly. *See also* **Point.**

Dry fly A fly that is designed to float on the surface of the water and tied using materials that will add to its buoyancy. Different patterns and styles of fly represent the various stages of life, and death, of flies that have hatched from nymphs.

Dubbing Both the materials, whether natural such as hare's fur or synthetic, and the process of applying them to the tying thread and winding it around the hook shank to build up a body when tying an artificial fly.

Dubbing needle A fine, sharp needle used to pick out dubbing fibres to represent the legs of a natural fly.

Dubbing wax Sticky wax used to help dubbing materials stick to the tying thread.

Duo Fishing a river with two flies, usually a combination of a dry fly with a nymph. *See also* **Trailer nymph**.

Emerger Refers both to a nymph in the act of hatching into a fly and an artificial fly designed to mimic this process.

False cast A forward and backward cast, or series of casts, keeping the fly in the air. Used to dry a wet fly, extend more line, or while waiting to make the final presentation cast.

Feeding lane A piece of water where noticeable quantities of food items are carried by the current.

Feeding lie Somewhere a fish can stay on station, using the minimum amount of energy, but close to a supply of food.

Ferrule The means of connecting together two sections of a rod, usually by pushing the end of one section into the other.

Fishing the water The process of casting to spots that you hope will hold a fish as opposed to casting to a rising or visible fish.

Floatant Material, in paste or liquid form, applied to flies and leaders to make them float on the surface of the water.

Floating line A fly line that is designed and manufactured to float on the surface of the water.

Forward cast When your rod and line are cast in front of you, towards your target. *See also* **Back cast** and **Presentation cast**.

Foul hook A fish is foul-hooked when it is hooked anywhere other than in its mouth.

Guide Someone who provides practical assistance and instruction for a day's fishing.

Guides Also known as rod rings which hold the fly line alongside the rod shaft. Not to be confused with more than one (fishing) guide.

Hackle A feather usually wrapped around the hook immediately behind the eye or, in the plural, feathers used to tie flies, from the neck or cape of a bird.

Hackle pliers Used to grip a hackle feather so that it can be held securely while being wound round a hook shank.

Hatch A hatch of flies happens when numbers of nymphs of the same fly hatch into adult, winged flies. There can also be multiple hatches when more than one type of fly is hatching.

Hooks Fly hooks are made with various shapes of hook bend and thickness of wire. The biggest hooks have the lowest size designation number and the smallest have the highest.

Indicator A device attached to, or part of, the leader, to indicate when a fish has taken a fly (nymph) fished below the surface.

Leader A tapered length of monofilament which connects the end of the fly line to the fly, usually with the addition of a sacrificial length of monofilament known as the tippet. Leaders can be either knotted, when lengths of different diameters of leader material are knotted together, or knotless when a leader is made from a single length of material, produced either by extrusion or acid immersion.

Leeward As in leeward or lee shore, the shore of a stillwater or lake onto which the wind is blowing. *See also* **Windward**.

Lie Where a fish spends most of its time in a river, usually a secluded or protected location close to a supply of food.

Line As in 'line a fish'. When a cast is made so that the fish sees the angler's line and is frightened by it.

Line hand The hand that holds and manipulates the fly line when casting and fishing. *See also* **Rod hand**.

Line weight Fly lines are classified by weight, to a standard system, based on the weight of the first 30 ft (9.1 m) of the line.

Load A rod is said to load, or be loaded, by making a series of back casts and forward casts which cause the weight of the fly line to bend the rod.

Long distance release What happens when you lose a good fish because the hook comes free, the tippet breaks or some other disaster strikes before you can release the fish yourself. Essentially losing a fish but then making the best of a bad job.

Match the hatch Anglers are said to be 'matching the hatch' when fishing an artificial fly that mimics as nearly as possible the natural flies that can be seen hatching.

Mend A mend, or mending your line, is when you use your rod to flip or move the line on the water surface, often upstream, to achieve a drag-free drift, or in such a way that a drag-free drift can be extended.

Monofilament Monofilament fishing lines, shortened to monofilament or mono, are made from a single fibre of plastic. They are cheap to produce, by extruding a mix of polymers, and are available in a range of diameters with different tensile strengths.

Nymph An artificial fly tied to represent the underwater, nymphal and/or larval stage of flies that are eaten by trout and other fish. Also the stage between the egg and the natural adult fly.

Parachute fly A fly with a hackle wound horizontally around a vertical post rather than vertically round the shank.

Parachute hackle A hackle wound horizontally around a vertical post.

Pin-on reel A spring-controlled device, with a cord or wire, to which tools are attached for quick and easy access. Usually pinned or clipped to a fly vest. Also known as a retractor, or sometimes a zinger.

Point The fly on the end of the leader when fishing with a team of two or three flies.

Pool An area of a river or stream with greater depth and slower current where fish are safer from predators and expend less energy in maintaining a safe lie.

Presentation The practice of placing a fly on or in the water where a fish would expect to see it, with delicacy and accuracy.

Presentation cast The final forward cast when your fly lands on or in the water.

Reel foot The part of the reel used to hold it to the **reel seat** on a fly rod.

Reel seat A fitting on the bottom end of the rod handle which holds the fly reel in place with sliding bands or rings tightened by a threaded locking ring.

Retractor *See* **Pin-on reel**.

Retrieve The process of recovering line after it has been cast, often in a specific way to impart the required movement to a fly.

Riffle A faster flow of water over small rocks, stone or broken water created by a convergence of two or more currents.

Rod hand The hand you use to hold your rod. *See also* **Line hand**.

Run A stretch of water often without any noticeable features, perhaps connecting one pool to another. Also when a hooked fish decides to get as far away from the angler as it can.

Saddle Feathers, attached to the skin, from the saddle area of a bird, used for fly-tying.

Scissors The corner of the jaws of a fish. Also a tool used for cutting fly-tying threads or tippet material.

Shooting line Shooting line involves releasing slack line as you stop the rod on the forward casting stroke to make a longer cast.

Sinking line A fly line designed to sink at a known rate measured in inches per second.

Sink(ing) tip A fly line where the tip (approximately the first 13 ft/4 m) only is designed to sink.

Spinner The final, mature stage of a fly's life. Female spinners lay their eggs on or in the water and male spinners die and often fall onto the water after mating.

Standing end The short area at the end of the standing part of the line. *See also* **Tag,** or **Tag end**.

Stillborn A fly that dies in the process of hatching.

Stock fish A fish that has been reared in captivity, in a fish farm, and then released into a river or lake in a process known as stocking.

Tag or **Tag end** The short end of any length of line that is subsequently cut or trimmed short.

Tailing loop Caused by a fundamental casting error when the business end of the fly line drops below the main line as a result of the rod tip following a concave path, rather than a straight path.

Tightening The act of raising the rod tip quickly to set the hook in the mouth of a taking fish.

Tippet A sacrificial length of monofilament, one end of which is attached to the end of the leader and the other to the fly. Attaching a tippet to the leader means that you do not have to cut and shorten your leader every time you change a fly.

Tippet material A general term covering all types of monofilament used for tippets.

Trailer nymph A trailer nymph is a nymph usually attached to the bend of the hook of a dry fly with a short length of monofilament. *See also* **Duo**.

Turn or wrap A turn or wrap is one complete revolution of one line around another.

Turn over Term used to describe how the fly line and leader straighten out on the completion of a forward, or presentation, cast.

Upstream The opposite direction to which a river is flowing. *See also* **Downstream**.

Weight forward A fly line with the bulk of its weight in the forward section, which then tapers into a smaller-diameter running line.

Whip-finish tool A device used to create a neat and secure finish to the head of a fly.

Wind knots *See* **Casting knots**.

Windward As in windward shore, the shore of a lake or stillwater from which the wind is blowing. *See also* **Leeward**.

Working end The part of the line used actively when tying a knot: the opposite of the standing end.

Zinger *See* **Pin-on reel**.

Index